Wings Above the Roof in 3-D

DANNY DELVALLE

PAGE PUBLISHING
Conneaut Lake, PA

First originally published by Page Publishing 2023

ISBN 978-1-64628-678-2 (pbk)
ISBN 978-1-64628-679-9 (digital)

Printed in the United States of America

I like to dedicate this book to my mother Beatrice Ramos Sanchez

1928–2007

CONTENTS

The weather is starting to change; fall is right around the corner. Corky is standing in front of the skylight wall with a white chalk in his hand, sketching an aircraft carrier on the wall with propeller planes flying off its deck. He names it *The USS Bombardier*. He writes the name on top. He turns around then says, "The roof is our carrier. The landing pad is the flight deck."

Ray says, "I can dig that, but your flight deck is crooked."

Corky looks at Ray. "Why you have to nitpick?"

Suddenly the song "Wendy" comes on the radio by the Association. Corky walks away from the skylight wall, saying, "He's going to name his next youngster Wendy." Ray says he is thinking the same thing, just to mess with them. "I was thinking the same thing too."

Corky says, "We can't have three Wendys flying around."

Ray says, "Okay, will shoot for it. The odd finger gets to name its next youngster—Wendy—."

So there they are, facing each other, Corky counting it off, "One…two…three—shoot!

—We are the Commanders of the SS Bombardier

CHAPTER 1

Wings Above the Roof in 3-D

It was a beautiful summer day, and I was driving on the Hudson Parkway going uptown. I was getting close to my old neighborhood. I looked down on my watch—I got time. I decided to drop by; it'd been a while. I got lucky and found a parking space not too far from the corner right across my old building, 1470. It was wonderful growing up in Manhattanville Project; they were spanking new when we moved in. It was a new beginning for everyone. I couldn't have asked for a better place to grow up. I exited my car and walked up the hill to the corner, looking at the store my friend Ray used to own. I turned, looking up at the roofs across the street. I was supposed to visit my friend in Jersey, but I had some time to spare. *Hey, there's my friend Wilson walking on the other side of the street.*

I called out his name, and he greeted me. "Hey, stranger." I waited for the green light and walked toward him. We shook hands and shoulder-bumped like in the old days. I asked him where everyone, and he said a lot of them moved away but there still a few left. After about ten minutes of talking, we exchanged phone numbers and said our goodbyes. I crossed the street and walked up the hill, looking up to the roof where my pigeon coop used to be on and remembering the excitement I had on that roof. Flying birds had to be one of the top ten best hobbies in the world. It's better than collecting stamps, that's for sure, and surely better than any video games that the kids are playing today.

"I got this urge to go up. There's a lot more traffic than I remember. Let me get away from this air pollution. I think I'll go up to the roof and get some fresh air."

"Good excuse, D."

I was bonded to that roof for five years; that roof was my world. I walked toward building 1492, and the door was locked and it was brand-new at that. I sat on the stoop, waiting for anyone to come out or go in. I saw a couple of familiar faces. I heard someone at the door, an elderly lady struggling to open the door with a shopping cart in her hand. I held the door open for her, and she looked at me and said thank you. Then she added, "I know you." I recognized her, but I didn't remember her name. "You're Danny. You were the one with those pigeons on the roof."

"Yes, that was me." I thought I was about to get scolded.

She said, "You know why I remember your name? Why, because of those news reporters asking me what stopped the traffic on Amsterdam Avenue. Out of all the people that were there that evening, they approached me, asking me questions about some strange-looking birds."

Some people claimed they saw something. Someone behind me was saying it looked like a bird from outer space, imagine that.

"Sorry about that," I said.

"That's okay, Danny. I got to see myself on TV, imagine that. I got my fifteen minutes of fame."

She had a big smile on her face. I told her I remember seeing her on the news that evening. "What did you say to the news reporters?"

"That a falcon was trying to catch a pigeon." She started laughing. "To tell you the truth, I wish I could've have said that. Actually, I told the news reporter that a big bird was trying to eat a little bird. Some people thought it was a bird from outer space, imagine that, but I found out later it was a falcon trying to catch a pigeon. Some kids up the block set the story straight."

"That was Stanley and Jerry," I told her. "We saw them on the news too. We were gone by the time the reporters came. We thought that we might be in some kind of trouble. We didn't want to bring attention to the super or the landlord." I also remember the fellas and me laughing at her interpretation of what happened.

"I don't expect you to remember my name. It's Maggie."

"Well, it's nice to meet you again, Maggie." As I turned to go in, she asked, "Where you going?"

"I'm going up to the roof to get some fresh air. I'll give you a hand with your groceries when you get back," remembering she lived on the fourth floor.

"That's nice of you," she said. "Being that you going to help me, I'll guess I get a little extra."

As I walked through the small hallway to the stairs, it was all coming back to me—six steps up, turn, six more, second floor. When I got to the fifth floor, passing apartment 5A, remembering my friend Carlos and Cassondra and their dog Peewee. I wonder how they were doing. I heard some noise up above; as I walked up to the skylight, I saw three kids sitting down, their heads buried in their phones. I said hello, and I was greeted with silence. I guess they don't talk to strangers. I pushed the door open, almost expecting to see the pigeon coop and the birds. It always seemed to be a little brighter on the roof.

I looked at the spot where my pigeon coop used to be and then walked to the front of the roof. You could see so much of the world from the roof it was like freedom for the eyes. The roof had its particular smell, which was the sweet smell of tar they used to waterproof the roof. Looking east toward Spanish Harlem, I didn't see any stock flying. I turned and looked up—nothing. Then I turned around toward riverside, not a single stock in the air. *Don't tell me that this hobby of mine does not exist anymore? What happened? Not one single stock as far as my eyes can see.*

I walked over to the small wall that separated the roof and sat. I guess this beautiful hobby went by the wayside, like all the beautiful games that we used to play as kids such as Johnny on the pony. Now that I thought about it, that was a tough game. All of a sudden, I noticed the kids were peeking through the door. I acted like I didn't notice. I could also hear them talking among themselves. Then the skylight door opened, and those three kids coming toward me asked me, "Is everything okay?"

"Yes," I said. "I'm just sitting here reminiscing."

"Reminiscing about what?" asked the young girl as her two friends were looking at me.

"I used to fly pigeons on this roof."

"Pigeons from the street?" asked one of the boys.

"That's funny. That's the same question I asked my friend Ray when he told me about his birds."

"Sorry that we didn't answer you when you said hello. We don't talk to strangers."

"Well, in that case, let me introduce myself. I'm Danny, but you can call me Mr. D. And your names are?"

"I'm Rachel," said the girl. She had a head full of long braids running down her shoulders. "But my friends call me Patty, and this is my brother David," she said, pointing to the smallest one in the group. Now pointing to the largest one, she added, "That's Joseph, but we call him Little Joe."

"Nice to meet you, Mr. D."

I was thinking to myself, nice name for a chubby kid. "Do you want to see a picture of my pigeon, Coop?" They all nodded in agreement. I pulled out my wallet and took the picture out and gave it to Patty as the boys came closer to look down on the picture.

"That's a nice pigeon house," said Patty.

"Did you build that by yourself?" asked David.

"No, I had help. Bring the picture closer. Do you see that bird? That's Sandy. Out of all the pigeons I ever had, she's my favorite."

"Did you name all your birds?" asked Patty. "No, only the special ones. There was Lucas, he was a tumbler, and Ripley, He was Sandy's brother."

"What's a tumbler?" asked David.

"It's a pigeon that does flips in the air while they're flying."

"Can a pigeon really to that?" asked Patty. I started rotating my two index fingers as they went around each other, trying to illustrate. "Tell us about Sandy," said Patty.

"No, Mr. D, tell us about the tumbler whose name is Lucas," said Little Joe.

"Lucas was amazing. The best tumbler in the world. For seven days, there was magic on this roof."

"What kind of magic?" asked David.

"The kind that comes from the heavens. Do you want to hear a good pigeon story?" All three of them said yes with their smiley faces. They slowly sat on the roof floor. "But I have to start from the beginning." They said okay but still messing around with a high-tech toy. Looking toward the sky, I began to share a wonderful part of my life with them.

"It was the night of the blackout, November 9, 1965. The lights went out at 5:27 p.m. I was fourteen when I met Ray."

"What's a blackout?" one of the boys asked.

"It's like when you turn off the light in your room when you're going to bed. I guess the electrical grid was overwhelmed. They said it was a transformer that blew out somewhere upstate. So the city was plunged into the darkness, and everything that was powered by electricity wasn't working, including the elevators in my building. The clock on the wall stopped ticking, and there was no TV. Now I was panicking. We happened to have a box of candles, and neighbors were knocking on each other's door, asking, 'What's going on?' In those days, we had small transistor radios, so we knew what happened.

"My mother shared her candles with everyone. My parents' names were Beatrice and Maxi, and my stepfather married my mother when I was very young. He was the only father I know. His old friends from the east side call him Big Red. Everybody else just called him Maxi, and they seemed to like him. Sometimes my mother used to send me out to get her coffee, and she would tell me to make sure the coffee looks like her complexion. If she's regular coffee, then Maxi was the cream."

Little Joe was laughing at my analogy. "Don't stop now," said David.

"I remember looking out the living room window from the eleventh floor. The lights were off on the George Washington Bridge, and I heard someone outside screaming 'Who turned off the lights?' My mother got her candles and lit them throughout the apartment.

I must admit it was scary and exciting at the same time looking at the candles flickering in the dark and everyone casting a shadow. It made the living room feel crowded. You never know how much you miss something until it was gone. My mother was telling us in Puerto Rico, the lights often went out for days. I guess that's why we had candles and our neighbors didn't. My father was telling us 'Let's hope the lights come on before the food in the refrigerator start to get spoiled.' My younger brother asked 'When will that be?' My father decided to go down to the store to get some canned food and purchase a couple of flashlight before the stores run out of them, if not some extra candles. 'We don't know how long this is going to last,' he said, 'so we better prepare ourselves.'

"We walked out of the apartment with six-inch white candles in our hands. Leaving my mother with my younger brother, I remember Pete saying 'Don't worry, Mommy. I will protect you' as he shadowboxed. 'Just keep the door locked,' he added as we walked out of the apartment. The hallway was dark as we walked toward the stairs. Opening the door to the stairwell, I saw that it was pitch-black. We heard footsteps up above now, seeing a light from a flashlight. Some of our upstairs neighbors were walking down. We joined them, still holding on to our candles. Going down the stairs, adults cracking jokes about walking back up. Reaching the first floor, walking out of the stairwell into a dark lobby and out the building. I'm sure everyone was hoping the stores were open. Walking toward the street, a parade of headlights was going both ways. The traffic was heavy, moving slow enough for us to get to the other side. All the stores were closing, seeing and hearing the owners shutting their gates after hearing rumors of looting. We were a little too late. The only store that was open on the block was the record shop. They seemed to have light. As we approached, looking through the window, the inside was lit up with lots of candles. It looked like they were open for business. I'd been inside a few times with my friends purchasing the latest 45s."

"What's 45s?" asked David.

"That's old school," said Little Joe. "They're small records. My mother played them once in a while." Little Joe just happened to be white with dark brown hair hanging from beneath his Yankee hat and with freckles on his round face. "Continue, Mr. D," he said.

"My father walked up to the front door, looking through the glass door and wondering why they were still open. I was behind him. We could see people inside, so he decided to go in and check on the owner, whom he happens to know from the old days at the Palladium where Spanish recording artists used to perform. I followed him in, and it was bright enough to see faces, and everyone brought their shadow with them. My father went to talk to the owner. She was at the far end of the counter, chatting with a couple of people that were there. Ray and Ellie were behind the counter, and you can tell they were related. I said hello, and they said hi. He introduced himself, 'I'm Ray and this is my sister Ellie.' Behind them were racks of 45s in their own little square cubicles and on the side two turntables that sit idle. Those two were messing around with the cards on the counter, and Ellie was looking at me in a strange way. She was speaking in a low voice, saying that her brother had magic powers. 'I'll bite, what kind of magic powers?' I asked. 'I'll prove it to you,' she replied. She was pointing to the cards that were on the counter, five cards on each side with three cards in the middle all facing up.

"She told me to pick as many cards as I want, and Ray would walk away and come back and tell me which ones I picked. When he came back, she started tapping every card a few times. I couldn't figure out how he did it. It didn't matter how many cards I picked, he would come back and pick my cards. I had them do it over and over again. It had something to do with the tapping of the cards. I pleaded with them to tell me the secret. Ray just started laughing and said no. He said it like I was asking for a million dollars.

"I looked toward my father's shadow stretching across the ceiling. He was over six feet tall and weighed about 230 pounds. I wonder why they called him Big Red. There was nothing red about his hair, it was light brown. Ray's mother said 'You can forget about the flashlights. They ran out of them as soon as the lights went out. I'm going to give you two so you can take it home with you. I seem to have a collection of flashlight, who would've known.' 'Thank you,' said my father. 'You're a lifesaver.'

"Then someone asked him if he wanted a drink. I walked away from the counter, disappointed that they didn't want to share the secret. It really was a neat trick I walked over to the front door and looked out. It was dark outside, and the only light I saw was coming from the cars' headlights, cars blowing their horns trying to navigate the intersection. To make the long story short, I went with Ray to his apartment. A few doors down, he had to pick up something for his mother. I don't quite remember what it was. So we walked out into the darkness. He had this big flashlight in his hands that cast a big beam of light, and down the hill we went. What I saw was long beams of light throughout the neighborhood. When we got to the front of his building, what I saw was a black tunnel. He led the way. The flashlight illuminated the hallway, and I could see the stairs.

"He lived on the second floor. His door was to the left, and he pushed the door open. As we were walking in, the lights came on. I looked straight ahead through the front windows and saw the lights were on in the streets. 'Let there be light,' said Ray. 'Thank God,' I said. His bedroom was next to the front door, and he invited me in. 'Have a seat, be right back.' His bed was against the wall, and he had this huge closet that extends from the wall opposite his bed. I noticed a lot of bird feathers at the bottom of his closet. The door was slightly open, so I took a peek. When he came back, I asked' him 'What's up with all the feathers in your closet?' He said he flies birds. 'Birds from the street?' I asked, and he replied no with a look on his face that told me he knows something that I don't know. 'No, my man. These birds cost money.'

"He walked to his bedroom window and lifted the window up. 'Take a look,' he said. I stuck my head out the window and saw a small roof adjacent to his window. 'My pigeon coop was on top of that roof.' He sounded a little sad. I asked him what kind of birds they were. He started rattling off names that I never heard of, like red flight, blue tiplit, homers, a Chinese owl. I told him I've heard of Homers, so I asked him what the difference between those birds. He said they all have different characteristics. He gave me an example between a homing pigeon and a flight.

"Homing pigeons are racing birds they take them far away hundreds of miles away and then they release them all at the same time. Whoever comes home first wins the race. He walked out of his bedroom, and I followed him into the living room. 'How do they determine the winner?' I asked. I took a seat on the couch, while he stood in the middle of the living room. The birds had a paper band on their leg, and the trainers were waiting to get the band off so he could clock it. Whoever has the best time wins the race. He seemed to enjoy telling me about the birds. Now on the other hand, the flight stayed close to their coop, flying around the roof. It stayed in its territory. Then he started mentioning tumblers, tail-sitters, and rollers. I was intrigued and amazed by what he was telling me.

"He said the tail-sitters sit on their tail feathers and come down, and tumblers, some assault while in flight and sometimes tumble all the way down and suddenly stop and fly back up again. He told me he had all kinds of birds in his stock. 'What's a stock?' I asked, and he replied 'Those are the birds that you own.' Then he mentioned a breed of birds called baldys. Right away I imagined that bird with no feathers on his head, which was not quite right. They come in solid colors but their heads got to be white. He said the black ones look like American Eagle. 'Why did you stop?' I asked, and he said the super made him take the pigeon coop off the small roof. The problem was that his coop was situated in the alley surrounded by brick walls and windows. The birds would land on everybody's windowsill on the way up to the roof. Then he walked up to the roof and chased the birds up.

"They would go around and around in circles. I was fascinated by his story. I continued asking questions, and he continued answering them. I asked him the next time he flies birds if I can I join him. He replied with a baffled look on his face, 'You don't know anything about flying birds.' I said, 'I know I don't, but I would like to learn.' He said it takes years to learn. I never brought it up again. But that night, we became friends.

"My friend Bronco, who lived on the fourteenth floor, started flying birds with Chickie, who lived on the first floor. From the back of my building, I could see them on the roof chasing their birds up from my window. I never gave it much thought. I was too busy play-ing stickball or running around with my friends. Once in a while, I used to catch Chickie coming in and out of the building with boxes of birds. Every time I did, I asked him if I can take a look inside the box. I was entering the seventh grade at 43 down the block. By the way, I graduated from the elementary school across the street P.S. 161."

"That's our school," Patty said and added that she'd be graduat-ing next year and was planning to go to 43.

"Good for you. Growing up around here was beautiful. Everything was so close by and walking distance from my home. I was excited starting the seventh grade there. I met a new friend. His name was Cornell Wade, like the actor."

"What actor?"

"That was a long time ago. Everybody called him Corky. He was a good friend. We were both in the same class together and on the swimming team. We used to go swimming every Wednesday eve-ning at P.S 129. In our many conversations, I happened to mention my friend Ray and the story that he told me about the pigeons. Now I know that pigeons are much more than just pigeons. To my sur-prise, Corky said he used to fly birds. 'Get out of town' I said and told him I would like to do that someday. He said he was thinking about doing it again. Then he asked me if I would like to fly birds with him. I said yes, of course, but I don't know much. I only know what Ray told me. Then he said 'You already know a lot more than the people in the street. I'll teach you what I know.'"

CHAPTER 2

Corky's Roof

"I was so excited I asked him if he knew of a roof we could fly birds on. He thought about it for a few seconds, and he said 'My roof. The super hardly goes up to the roof.' I told him 'Because she doesn't have a reason to.' He replied 'Believe me, they're too busy taking care of all the buildings they have.' I know the super, she's small in size and skinny and mean. Every time I see her, she seemed to have a broom in her hand. She and her husband take care of three buildings around the corner from Corky. If she finds out that we are on one of her roofs, she would definitely kick us off—I mean kick us off the roof! Corky knows how mean she is. Between her and her husband, she's the enforcer.

"After school, we went up to Corky's roof after spending some time in his apartment. He closed his door and led the way up. The last stairs ended at the roof door, and it was dark. He lifted the latch, and we found ourselves on the roof. I'll never forget how bright it was. I walked to the front, looking over the ledge down to the street and seeing the entire block from above. Cars were neatly parked, pointing toward Amsterdam Avenue across the street Annunciation church. It's beautiful. I noticed Corky's roof was attached to Knickerbocker Hospital by a brick wall with two windows high above. I walked to the back of the roof, looking down, and to the left, you could see the emergency entrance to the hospital. There's a thin tall wall and on the other side the back side of four buildings, a huge backyard. I see clothe lines connected to wooden poles. Every building had one, and they ran the length of the backyard. I could see the top of their roof.

"In the opposite direction 1470 my building, which stands twenty-story high with a water tower sitting on top of it, I could see my balcony on the eleventh floor. To my right, I discovered a brand-new highway. The buildings were connected to each other on a downslope. When I turned around, Corky was reaching for the handle on the dumbwaiter door. The dumbwaiter extends from the basement all the way up to the roof, and I saw the dumbwaiter door in his kitchen. He pulled on the handle of this rusty door, and it opened. Then he turned to look at me, saying 'We don't have to build a pigeon coop. We already have one made.' I walked over to this rusty door and took a look inside, the elevator looking like an empty box. It stuck on top of the roof.

"It was dirty and dusty with a lot of spiderwebs. The tenants used to put their bags of garbage inside and send it down to the super to collect. We got some soap and water from his apartment and we cleaned it up real good. 'This is perfect,' said Corky. 'Now we don't have to worry about your friend with the broom finding a pigeon coop on the roof.' We both thought it was a slick idea."

"Was the dumbwaiter run by electricity?" asked Patty.

"No, rope and pulley. We were planning to build a coop with milk crates, which was made out of wood at the time. They could be found in front of any store, waiting for the milk company to pick them up."

My first pigeon coop, the dumbwaiter

"Corky shut the dumbwaiter door, and we started talking about buying birds that coming Friday. We would both be getting our allowances. It seemed like it took forever for Friday to come. We took our twenty dollars and headed down toward Spanish Harlem toward 116th Street on Second Avenue. Corky been there many times before. This will be my first time going in there, and it wouldn't be my last. From the outside, it looked like a regular pet shop. We walked in, and the owner was behind the counter. His name was Mike. Corky told him 'We want to buy some birds.' He asked Corky 'Do you know about the blackboard?' and Corky said yes. 'Okay,' said Mike, 'there in the back waiting for you.' Corky knew the direction. On our way there, we passed a tank with a beautiful tropical fish blowing bubbles. Pretty canaries in their cages and one big parrot saying his name is Tarzan. I asked Corky what the blackboard was for. He said that's where they post upcoming events. I must admit I was excited. The door had a window, and I saw wooden cages. Corky opened the door, and there they were, all types of birds. There were four different stalls made out of wood and poultry netting, which I called chicken wire.

"Each stall had a different price, the highest was ten dollars. We chose the four-dollar stall. There were two boys inside the holding pen taking the birds they wanted, and we had to wait. There must be about fifty birds inside the holding pen. Corky already had his eyes on a bird he wanted. He was hoping it wouldn't be picked, and it wasn't. After they were finished, the owner came in and counted the birds and put them in boxes. When it was our turn to go inside the pen, Corky gave me a quick schooling about the birds that were there. Corky told me flights have pink beaks and tiplit have dark beaks. I saw all kinds of different colored birds. I saw a baldy that Ray told me about. I saw a bird in the corner going around in circles, dipping his head, and spreading his tail feathers. I asked 'What's wrong with that bird?' and Corky said 'He's bugging.' I asked him 'Is he crazy?' and Corky started laughing. 'He's not crazy. That's his courtship dance. He's trying to get a girlfriend.' Corky was pointing to individual birds and giving me the names and the colors that they go by.

"Some birds had different color bands on their leg. I managed to catch a few to check out, and some had metal band with the date of birth. I noticed the homers were a little larger than the rest of the birds. The majority of the homers were grayish blue. I soaked up as much information as I could. The birds were flying all over the place. Corky picked two flights, one was red and the other was yellow. Their wing tips were white. I also picked two birds, one was a tiplit, which was white with dark feathers sprinkled around its body and a blue flight with white tips.

"I noticed that the flights had light-colored eyes. Mike, the owner, was probably wondering what was taking us so long. He came with the medium-sized box, and Corky opened the door to the holding pen and passed the birds to Mike. 'I did the same,' he told me. 'I picked out a good Canadian tiplit. Those birds are smart,' he said. With the remaining four dollars, we bought pigeon food and carried the box all the way to Corky's roof. I have my first two birds. You can learn a lot at the pet shop. You see other flyers from all over the city. You listen to the conversation, each of them has a story to tell about their birds. I even learned how to tell the difference between young birds and old birds. Old birds will have larger crusts on their beaks, and younger birds will have none. It's difficult to tell between male and female. You find out when one of them starts doing his courtship dance, that would be the male. On our way home, Corky was telling me that we wouldn't have to buy birds anymore. He said we were going to build our stock by catching strays."

"What's a stray?" asked little Joe.

I told him, "It's a bird that is lost, so the more strays you catch, the bigger your stock gets. We built the holding pen the day before. Surrounded by chicken wire, it was three feet high and five feet across with a small opening on top. The whole thing will be lifted to let the birds out. We had a small pot filled with water and a plate filled with pigeon food. The first day, I stood on the roof all day watching them. I noticed my blue flight and Corky's red flight were males. I saw them bugging on my Canadian and Corky yellow flight. By the second day, it was getting boring just watching them inside the pen.

"The only thing that was exciting was catching them and putting them back inside the dumbwaiter when it got dark. We didn't let anyone know what we were doing. It was our secret. Sometimes we would leave the birds on the roof and go play basketball. The temptation to let them out was so great. We were going to keep them in for four days. But we couldn't wait any longer, so on the third day early in the morning, it was the big day. It was a nice day. We put them in the box-shaped screen for a little while. Later on, we lifted the box screen, and they stood there on the roof floor for a few seconds. Wondering what happened to the screen, we made sure the dumbwaiter door was open. That's where they slept. That's their home. They flew right into the dumbwaiter for a few seconds and back to the roof floor. Corky said that was a good sign, and then he chased them up.

"I really wanted them to stay on the roof a little longer. They circled around the roof. It was intense, and I was hoping they didn't fly away. We purposely didn't feed them. Corky practically emptied out the bag of pigeon food, whistling and tossing the food on the roof to get their attention to come down. They just kept flying and gliding around the roof and over Knickerbocker Hospital. I wonder how long they'd been in the pet shop. I was excited, and it was beautiful to watch. When I was a kid, I remember going to Pala Bay Park and watching these guys with their gasoline-driven small planes held by the strings that the person holds in his hand. The plane went around in circle, and the person holding the string was also going around in circles.

"I had no strings, that was the coolest thing about it. I looked up and saw they started to fly together. All four birds were flying in unison around the roof. They looked like small planes to me. I have a fascination with World War II fighter planes and the pilot wearing their goggles. They looked so cool. When they finally landed on the roof, what a relief, boy, we were happy I think I got little carried away with excitement. Corky told me to cool it. I forgot we didn't want anyone to know we were on the roof. 'Sorry about that' I said. There were other flyers beside Chickie and Bronco. In the hood, there was Stanley and Jerry on Amsterdam Avenue, and Choo-Choo and Danny boy were between Amsterdam and Broadway on 135th. They got over two hundred birds. And on 135th on Riverside Drive, they had a lot of birds too. I decided I'd get to know those guys later."

"Did the super ever found out you had pigeons on one of her roofs?" asked Patty.

I thought Patty was really paying attention. "Yes, she did, she came up one afternoon." "Corky and I were on the roof sitting on the wall that separates the buildings. We heard the skylight door opening, and it was the super, and she had her broom, the kind of broom we used to play stickball with. I was hoping she just finished sweeping the stairs or she was carrying it to beat us upside our heads with it. Corky and I already discussed what we were going to do if she came up to the roof. We were going to act normal.

"What she saw was two teenagers having a conversation. She has known Corky since he was a little kid. Corky had tried flying pigeons on her roofs before, and she doesn't allow that. Our birds were up in the air, and we were hoping they don't come down. She was definitely investigating, thinking she must have seen the pigeons on the ledge. She walked around, acting like she wasn't really looking for anything. What she was really doing was looking for sign of a pigeon coop. The dumbwaiter door was close. She asked us 'What are you doing up here?' Corky told her 'We're just talking and getting some fresh air.' She slightly nodded. Then she jumped on her broom, and the skylight door magically opened, and up and down she went. I found out later she would go up to the roof at night looking for evidence of a pigeon coop. Corky's idea of using the dumbwaiter as a pigeon coop was perfect.

"The secret was out the bag. When you're first starting out, it is the most dangerous time. Your birds can easily be pulled into a flying stock and never come out. Now every flyer in the hood knows someone is trying to start up a new stock. Our four birds triggered the flyers to chase their birds up, trying to capture our four birds. On the back side of my building were Chickie and Bronco. Bronco was my first friend when we first moved into this new project. I gave him the nickname Bronco while playing Scalise in the balcony. We remained friends until his passing. He would be the first one to chase up, and the rest will follow. The only time we saw their birds was when they were flying higher than my building. From 125th Street to 135th Street is one big hill.

"We were farther down the hill. Most of the time, our birds would disappear over my building. Looking uptown, we couldn't see Stanley and Jerry roof, but we could see their birds when they were up in the air. Sometimes our birds would be gone for a long time. Looking uptown, toward the sky, we would sit and wait, looking at each other and saying 'They caught our birds.' After a while keeping our fingers crossed and saying our silent prayers, we would see our birds coming back from their excursion. Seeing them coming back home made me happy. The flyers in the hood, they were already talking about our four birds."

"What is Scalise?" asked Little Joe.

"It's a game that we played on the floor with bottle tops. We would draw a large square box on the floor, and within the box, there were small square boxes with numbers from one to twelve. Whoever got to twelve first wins the game. We used our fingers to push the bottle tops around. Ray came up a couple of times. He was surprised how much I've learned. We only lasted two months. One day, our birds were gone. Someone had stolen our birds. We didn't have a lock on the dumbwaiter door, easy picking, lesson learned. It broke my heart.

"That evening, my mother told me 'Someone saw you playing on the roof.' I didn't know what to say. By me keeping my mouth shut, I was guilty as charged. 'The roof is no place to be playing games. It's dangerous, you hear me? Stay off the roof, or else I'll be punished.' I told her okay, thinking I gotta be more careful. Flying birds have seeped into my soul. I had this beautiful blue suit that my dad bought me for graduation. I wore the pants to school, and after school, I went up to the roof and got tar on my pants, which my mother noticed. I was tired of ducking and hiding every time I thought my mother was on the balcony, looking to see if I was on the roof. So for the first time, I spoke up for myself, trying to defend my new hobby. She asked me what I was doing on the roof, and I told her I was flying birds with my friend Corky and that I really like what I'm doing. 'I don't want you on the roof,' she said, and I replied 'But, Mom, I don't lean over the edge. We use a long bamboo stick to chase the birds up.' Actually, it was a long mop stick. 'I don't want you on that roof!'

"At the same time my father was walking by, saying his cousin Joey used to fly birds in Spanish Harlem—touché—she looked at him with burning eyes. I pleaded with her, 'Mommy, I love what I'm doing. Plus I have birds that belong to me on that roof.' 'Okay, I'll go up there with you.' I remember Ray and I wanted to go night fishing at the Hudson, and she wouldn't let us go by ourselves. She had to tag along. 'I am not going to fall off the roof. That would be an embarrassment for a pigeon flyer.' 'You won't be embarrassed,' she said. 'You'd be dead.' I was trying to convince my mother that I was mature enough to be on the roof without supervision.

"I must've taken her by surprise. By the way, I was sticking up for what I was doing. She stood there looking at me for a few seconds, and then she grabbed me and started hugging me and kissing me, one long one on my forehead, and told me to be super careful and not to embarrass myself. 'And come home first and change your clothes,' she said. 'Thank you, Mom.' I didn't tell her that someone stole our birds.

"During that day, Corky and I were angry. We were going to visit every coop in the neighborhood. We eliminated Chickie, as he just recently moved to The Bronx and took his birds with him. So the first stop, Stanley and Jerry, they were the closest coop. We didn't go any farther. When we walked onto the roof one building over, they were surprised to see us on the roof, asking what was up. As we got closer, Corky told them someone tapped us last night. Tapping means that someone broke into your coop and stole your birds. The brothers didn't seem to look guilty.

"We all have seen each other around the neighborhood but never really spoken. They've been living in this neighborhood since they were kids. I looked over to their roof, seeing a lot of birds. 'I'm Jerry,' he said. I took my eyes off the pigeons. He was the tallest of the two, and that my brother Stanley. Corky told them our names. 'I think I see a stray,' said Stanley, and we all looked up. He picked up a red flag on a long stick. Walking toward his birds, he whipped it downward, making a loud snapping sound. His birds took off.

"Stanley told us we were welcome to take a look inside their coop. Corky and I already knew they didn't take our birds. We told them that was okay. We looked at their coop, a big box, and it was silver-looking and covered in tin with a nice-sized entrance to enter. I asked them how many birds they have. 'Close to a hundred,' said Stanley with his brown hair hanging down to his ears. When I met Jerry and Stanley, I was impressed with the way they handled their stock.

"I was in no hurry to go, watching their birds fly high over our heads, tail-sitters doing their thing, and tumblers tumbling. Jerry was telling us 'If anybody around here stole your birds, they will be back because those birds were bad! Nobody could bring them down. they flew above everybody's stock.' Hearing those words coming from Jerry's mouth made me feel proud. 'You're right about that, Jerry,' I said and Corky agreed with me. I was sad and angry. I guess I must've brought my disappointment to the dinner table my mother asked me 'What's wrong?' I replied 'I might be catching a cold or something.'

She quickly placed her hand on my forehead and said 'You are a little warm. Let's see how you feel tomorrow. I'm cooking pasteles tomorrow.' That put a little smile on my face.

"That evening, I was lying in bed thinking the day they stole my birds was the day I got permission to be on the roof. Finally falling asleep, I had the strangest dream, that a large pigeon was hovering over me while I lay in bed, fanning me with her wings. I reached up to touch it, but it was out of my reach. My arms started to grow longer, but I still couldn't touch it, and it was just right there. When I woke up that morning, I was soaked in sweat. The pasteles was delicious, but the birds never came back.

"During that summer, Ray got to know Corky very well. We played softball and stickball and we would go downtown to the movies together. I remember we saw *The Dirty Dozen* together. We were mad that Jim Brown died in the movie. Being that we were pigeon flyers, we decided to fly together the three amigos. Corky's roof became off-limits for us. The building on Convent Avenue had big skylights. We tried to get slick and put one row of milk crates on top of the skylights. I remember we would sometimes have to lie down flat when someone came up to the roof to investigate. Every summer, we would fly birds, something that we just had to do, but we always managed to get kicked off either by the super or the landlord."

"What happened to the birds when you got kicked off the roof?" asked David.

"They would go join the other stocks in the neighborhood. Once we stopped feeding them, they would become strays and let themselves get caught because they were hungry and probably thirsty."

CHAPTER 3

The Roof

"I had a friend who lived in this building on the fifth floor apartment 5A. His name was Carlos, and he had a sister named Cassondra, who was cute. Because of him, I got to know the super, who was a tough fella from Mississippi who likes to drink his moonshine on the weekends. His nickname was cut, and it stood for 'I'll cut you if you mess with me.' I liked him, he really was a good person. Anyway, one night, as I was walking down the hill from Carlos's building, I found him in a very good mood. I asked him if my friends and I can fly pigeons from his roof. To my surprise, he said yes. Thank God for the moonshine. He said under one condition, that we sweep and mop the stairs and help with the garbage on Saturdays and Sundays. I thought to myself, that's three, no, that's four conditions. I said no problem. We were up there during the summer of '67, and by this time, we were pretty good at building coops, as we saw enough of them.

"We often visited other flyers in the neighborhood and checked out their coop. There was a new building going up in city college. With the help from our young proteges, who would always follow us around when we were in the streets, we started building the coop. They helped us get the material from the dumpster. We would do this at night. Those knuckleheads always made us laugh. There were also a few abandoned buildings in the neighborhood. The windows were covered with tin.

"We took four sheets of tin from the windows. We nailed the tin to the frame, and we got lucky there was a bucket of tar and a row of tar paper, which was left inside the skylight. The roof was recently done. The super told us not to nail anything to the roof floor. We smeared the tar all over the coop and then wrapped it with the tar paper and secured it with flathead nails. This will keep the rain and the snow out. It really was a messy job. We all ruined our clothes that day. We built another coop, as the stock got bigger. It wasn't much to look at, but it was strong. We painted both coops red. The frame of the holding pen was painted white and painted red on top, but we really outdid ourselves in building the screen with two trapdoors. It was pretty to the eyes.

"The screen was also called holding pen. The frame was made out of two-by-fours nailed together, and then we wrapped chicken wire around it. The trapdoor is to the left at the bottom and the other to the right on top.

Picture of pigeon coop with fluffy clouds.
Those are the fluffiest clouds ever—looks like cotton candy.

This picture is from the top of the skylight and the
roof of the public school across the street.

"In this picture is Corky with his big Afro with his chest puffed
up, looking like a proud peacock. In the background is music and
arts high school. You can see the open sky that I talk about, and you
could see some birds on the landing pad, which is the edge of the
roof. We always kept a clean roof. I have many fond memories being

on that roof with my friends, and I loved every minute of it. Down at the bottom is Ray posing in front of the store on the corner. He would often step out of the bodega to watch the birds fly. I felt bad for him. He wanted to be on the roof. He loved the birds as much as I did. He would come up to the roof during his brakes and sometimes sneak away for a few minutes, which he did often."

When I was pointing to the music and arts high school
that Gothic-looking building to the left, the kids
said, "The school is no longer called music and arts.
It's called Philip Randolph High School." To make a
long story short, the lights came on the next day.

CHAPTER 4

The Basement

"Ray heard about this place in Bay Chester in The Bronx, where the owners of the pet shops purchased their new birds to sell. We ventured out and took the train to Bay Chester Avenue. This place was huge, and it looked like a supermarket for birds. We saw all kinds of birds in holding pens, parrots, finches, canaries. We went to the pigeon section. The foundation of our stock would be Canadians. I convinced the fellas that they are the smartest birds on the planet. We bought twenty of them. Most of them had multicolored feathers—brown, white, black—all over their bodies, and a few were grayish-looking. They'd never been on the roof, and they smelled like baby powder. They were all young, and we were going to give them their first home.

"So fresh, so clean. It took us three years to get to this point, and now we have a roof and a beautiful coop. And The two Irish brothers up the block, Stanley and Jerry, yeah, we lost a few birds to them in the beginning. Being so close made it exciting, and being so close to the top of the hill, now we could see the three stocks in Spanish Harlem. The second year of us being on the roof, when the weather turned cold, I asked the super if we could take the birds down to the basement for the winter. He said yes but under one condition. I thought, here we go again, if you and your friends clean up the basement for me, believe me that was not an easy job. First, we had to get rid of the cats. They gave us a hard time. We chased them out the door one by one. There was so much useless stuff down there. By this time, we had about eighty birds.

"We collected as much milk crates as we could and took them down to the basement and stacked them up in a horseshoe pattern and surrounded it with chicken wire. It had a door to go in and out, and we made it cat-proof as much as possible. We were going to breed birds for the first time. We brought nesting bowl from the pet shop and put one in every milk crate. Within weeks, eggs started to appear inside the bowls. Many times I sat there and watched the parents taking turns laying on the eggs. It took about seventeen to twenty days for the chicks to emerge. Those poor things struggled trying to poke a hole through the shell. Watching them come into this world was pretty cool. The babies were born yellow down with a light pink beak. The baby birds are called squads. What the parents fed them is called crop milk, digestive juices from the food that the parents ate."

David raised his hand and asked, "How do the parents feed the baby squabs the juices?"

"On a plate with a fork and knife," Patty said with such a straight face. David had a confused look on his face.

"Come on, David," said Little Joe. "You've seen how birds feed their babies."

"Oh yeah."

I couldn't stop laughing. Now they were laughing at me. "Okay, give me a few seconds. I took a deep breath. It felt good to laugh. "Okay, where was I?"

"Baby birds," said David.

"Yes, baby birds. The squads are fed by both parents. The parents don't like me reaching inside the bowl, especially when there are eggs in the bowl. They will quickly wing-slap you and it hurts. It's like snapping a towel. If you touch the eggs too much, they won't sit on them. There was an old radio, and we always kept it on. These chicks are going to have some rhythm and blues in their blood. I never thought that someday we'd be breeding birds. It's interesting to watch, from eggs to flight. You develop an interest in these youngsters, which is really cool. They get to know you, you get to know them, and you develop a love for them. Being down in the basement, I was worried about the cats in the alley trying to get back in. I often heard them fussing and fighting. I was hoping that they never get in.

"I was fascinated by the whole process. I spent most of my free time with the birds, and I didn't look from the outside of the pen. I had to be inside the pen with them. After the commotion of me being inside, they would settle down. I'd sit on the water can and just watch them go about their business. I mostly looked at my birds. We all have our favorite, but there was something special about this group. They seemed more animated being in the basement. It was amazing. I swear it looked like they were talking to each other, and they probably were. They would visit each other's nesting bowl when an egg had hatched. My birds wore a yellow band, and Corky was green, Ray with red.

"The females usually lay two eggs. If Nova found a mate with a green or red band, I'd get one egg, and whoever it was got the other. We all took turns caring for them while they were down in the basement. Most of the time the fellas would find me there. I was happy when Nova, my Canadian' grizzle, and Clyde, another Canadian grizzle, became a pair."

"The Canadians are from Canada," said Patty. "The name speaks for itself, right?" She was trying to convince me.

"Well, Nova lost her mate to the Dutchman that summer. I lost a beautiful red owl with a white body with red wings and a cap on his head with a pink beak. He really stood out among the birds. They supposedly originated from China.

"Who's the Dutchman?" asked Little Joe, pointing toward the city college.

"His birds were on the other side of the park on 135th. He was the super of the building on the corner. I admire him. No matter how old you are, you can always fly birds. I remember the first time I saw the Dutchman, he was white and tall, wearing blue strap corduroys and was tough-looking in his sixties. We rang the super bell, and he opened up the door. We told him we wanted to buy some birds. Anybody who flew birds, one time or another, bought birds from the Dutchman. He was a legend in our neighborhood. The rumor was that he used to be a gangster in the old days. He let us in, and we took the service elevator. He pushed the gate to the right, down to the basement, and then he had to pull the gate to the left in order for us get out. He led us down this long corridor. It was spooky the first time, and we were hoping we didn't see any skeletons. We came upon a large room where he had a big holding pen with over one hundred birds inside. He told us 'Take your pick.' He didn't care. They were all of the same price, three dollars. No matter how long we kept his birds inside our coop, they always flew back to him, but that didn't stop us from buying bird from him. Yes, the Dutchman. And nobody ever caught his birds, and I mean *nobody*. Now my favorite birds are Canadian tiplets ever since I had my first one. She left an impression on me. They're just as smart as homing pigeons, if you ask me.

"Those Canadians, they could stay up in the air for hours. They're strong flyers and very loyal. Give them a good home, they'll stay forever. When our stock was flying and they reached a certain height, a bunch of them would fly out of our territory. It's called ripping, and they caused so much havoc."

"What do you mean?" asked David.

"What I mean by havoc is that they create so much fun and excitement for the other flyers around the city. They would chase their birds up, trying to snare our birds and bring them down to their roof. Our birds flew higher by the time their birds got up to speed, and our birds were gone. Our birds flew uptown, downtown, across town, no territory was off-limits to them. And the excitement we felt when they were coming back home, it made us proud."

Patty asked, "Do birds communicate with each other?"

"I think all living animals have a way of communicating. I often found myself talking to Sandy, but I like to think she knew what I was saying. Down in the basement—"

"Did she talk back to you?" asked David.

"No, but I felt there was a strong connection between us, just like the connection I have with my longtime girlfriend. She's always off to see the world. She reminds me of Sandy in so many ways. I know this is going to sound crazy, but sometimes I think…never mind. Where was I? Oh, down in the basement, there was a commotion at the bottom of the holding pen on the basement floor. Nova was tending to her two chicks, Ripley and Sandy, while Clyde was standing on the edge of the crate, looking down. Nova heard panic among the birds and asked Clyde what was going on. 'I think a chick fell out his bowl,' said Clyde. 'That's horrible,' said Nova. 'Why don't you go down and see?' She watched Clyde leap off the milk crate. With two flaps of his wings, he was on the floor as he pushed his way through the crowd of birds toward the baby bird lying on the basement floor. His name is Lucas, and his parents are by his side. Lucas was trying to stand upright, but he kept falling down. Clyde looked up to see where he fell from. One crate higher he might've crippled himself. Clyde turned to leave, and with his two strong wings, he majestically lifted himself up straight up to Nova. She asked 'Is the chickie okay?' 'He'll be fine. Thank God for soft bones,' said Clyde, 'but he has a big bump on his head.' Clyde, turning around, heard a loud voice. It was Rufus shouting 'For those who are parents, let that be a lesson to all of you. Keep an eye on your chicks. You know they love to move around. Clyde, he cannot stay down there. It's not safe.'

"Clyde saw the concerned look on Nova's face. 'Don't worry. One of the trainers will put him back in the bowl." Right there and then, the basement door suddenly opened. It was Ray taking a lunch-break from his job at the corner store. Ray walked into the holding pen to get the water can. All the pigeons flew back to their crates, except two birds on the floor who stood by a baby bird lying on its side. He asked the squab what he was doing there and gently picked up the squab and put him back in his nesting bowl. He was the only single chick among the baby birds. The two pigeons followed. A few minutes later, Corky and I entered the basement, and I told Ray there was a cat hanging around the front door. The cat ran off when he saw us. We did some housecleaning and made sure everything was secure.

"We would always leave the radio on, hoping that any intruder would think there was someone with the birds. When a song that we knew came on the radio, we would start singing. The birds seemed to get happy. I like to think they were singing along with us. As time went by, the youngsters' flight feathers were growing fast. Clyde could see all the youngsters flapping their wings in a nesting bowl. Soon it would be time for school as soon as they could fly down and fly back up again. Rufus was nominated to do the teaching. He was the keeper of the books, and Sarge held the title of commander.

"Clyde looked up toward Sarge, who was perched high above, remembering the time Sarge got caught by Ray when we first came up to the roof. He was the first stray to join us. He has traveled a long road. He taught us how to fly tight. He was a natural born leader. Looking at all the happy families, I thought this was a good thing, as it bonded us even more. These youngsters had an advantage that most of us didn't have, time to learn to fly right, and now I was a proud father of two youngsters, Ripley and Sandy. There was something special about Sandy. I couldn't put my feather on it, and Ripley seemed to have good common sense, which he must have gotten from me as time went by. The youngsters are now off the parents' milk. The trainers have removed all the nesting bows from the crates. They are now feeding on pigeon food, which consist of corn, hops, peas, and barley. Sandy and Ripley asked their father, who was named after Danny's favorite basketball player.

"'Tell us about the roof, again,' said Clyde. 'Yes, Father. Tell us about the son and the blue skies and the beautiful white clouds and don't forget about the coop.' 'Soon you will see it for yourselves. It is time for school now, so get ready.' All the youngsters gathered down at the bottom of the basement floor, where Rufus was holding class in front of an open crate with the blackboard in the back. He had the attention of all the youngsters and started off by saying, 'You must follow the adults when we're flying, and to fly in a tight group, we fly with the wind and hook. When we are against it, do not to fly off on your own.' Rufus pointed to the blackboard to show us one maneuver we should not play with, and it was called the inverted loop, which puts too much strain on the wings. He said, 'You might end up with a bum wing, or worst-case scenario, broken wing bones. This is to be used only in emergencies. It may buy you time to get away.'

"As he points to an illustration of a hawk chasing a pigeon you must go up to pull it off to complete the loop, he said, 'You must go up and over, and you will find yourself flying upside down. But you must continue to go down as fast as you can. It would help you put a distance between you and the hawk. Your parents will fill you in about the dangers that await us above the roof.' Rufus was interrupted by a youngster named Penny.

"'Is it true that crows eat baby birds?'

"'Yes, if given a chance, but you're no longer a baby.'

"Another youngster named Bingo said, 'Is it true that falcons are the fastest birds in the sky?'

"'Yes,' said Rufus. 'Falcons attack from above they can hit speed of two hundred miles an hour on a steep dive and snatch you right out the sky.'

"'Wow,' the youngsters said in unison.

"'There are other dangers. There are three stocks in our hood, and one is nearby. Do not pay them any mind and always keep your eyes on the leaders. There is a trainer named the Dutchman, and he lives across the park. You must never land on his roof. We lost a dear friend to him last summer. We don't know how he did it. We saw our friend go down, and he never came back home again.'

"'Did the Dutchman eat him?' someone asked.

"'He doesn't eat us. He catches birds and sells them. We see our friend flying with their birds.'

"'Why doesn't he come back?' asked Sandy.

"'We think he likes it there.'

"One of the birds hollered out, creeping at the window. Everyone was looking at the bottom of the window and saw that it was that gray cat again with two friends looking in. And all of a sudden, they disappeared. The basement door opened up.

"'Did you see those cats run when they saw us?' said one of the fellas. All three trainers were carrying empty boxes, which they put neatly against the basement wall. That was the signal that the birds had been waiting for. Seeing the boxes, Rufus said, 'Class dismissed,' and the youngsters flew back up to their parents. The trainers cleaned up a bit. Corky told me that he was going up to the roof with Ray to do some repairs on the coop. When they left, I walked into the holding pen and sat down on the water can, just watching the birds. Rufus told Sarge, 'I need more time with the young birds,' and Sarge replied, 'Schedule another class after the trainers leave.' Rufus nodded his head.

"I gave them fresh water and food. I was starting to rise up from the water can when Lucas jumped off the top crate and tumbled down, two complete loops all way down to the floor, landing on his feet. Lucas was a tumbler, what a crazy thing to do in such a confined space.

"Sandy hollered, 'Out you go, Lucas.' Then she asked her brother, 'Did you see that?'

"'Yes, I saw it.'

"'If he doesn't watch out, he's going to crack his head again.'

"'He didn't crack his head. It was just a bump.' Then Ripley asked, 'Sandy, do you like him?'

"'I think he's cute.' Thinking, she added, *But not as cute as D.*

"I walked out the holding pen. Corky had a tumbler, and I couldn't wait to tell them what I saw. I headed up to the roof. Rufus was at the bottom of the floor, telling all the youngsters to come down. 'We have a lot to cover.' All the youngsters started moaning. Nova told Ripley and Sandy, 'It's important that you get all the knowledge you can because it might save your life someday.'

"'Okay, Mom.' They flew down to the basement floor.

"Rufus told us about the dangers of getting caught by other trainers and the tricks they used to snatch us up. He also told us about the water can and the trapdoors. Rufus went silent for a few seconds, and then he asked, 'Is there any predators here?'

"'No,' said the youngsters in unison.

"'That's because they are out there in the sky waiting for you to make a foolish move, like straying away from the stock.' He continued, 'There's a lot of different birds flying around, big ones and small ones. Sparrows are the smallest birds out there, and they're friendly. Keep your eyes on the big ones. They are called eagles, and we rarely see them. There are also hawks, falcons, ravens, and chickie hawks, which are smaller but act like full-grown hawks, sometimes making a fool out of itself.' Rufus was drawing pictures of all the birds of prey on the blackboard. 'We live next to the Hudson River,' he said as he drew a picture of a seagull, 'and they eat fish. Many times they're mistaken for a bird of prey. There's a water tower nearby.' Rufus drew the picture and then added, 'If you're ever lost, look for the water tower. Now I'll have Sarge, who is our commander, give you a history lesson about our kind.' All the youngsters were looking at Sarge with respect. He had a burned-out match stick under his wing.

"He started off by saying that birds have been around for millions of years and that they have helped mankind in many ways. One of the youngsters raised his wing, but Sarge didn't like being interrupted. 'HI, I'm Ripley.' Ripley saluted Sarge, and Sarge saluted back. 'I know who you are. What's your question, Ripley?' 'How did we help mankind?' asked Ripley. 'I was getting to that before you interrupted.' Sarge started pacing back and forth in front of the class. 'Well, let me begin by telling you a story that my father told me and his father told him and so forth. It was during the time of war between human beings. I don't know why they fight, but they do sometimes. The armies used pigeons, just like us, sending them home with valuable messages in a small canister attached to their legs, flying across vast distance of land. The enemy soldiers on the ground tried to shoot them down, if that wasn't enough, on the now English Channel, which is one million times wider than our Hudson River. Enemy planes could not stop them. Those courageous pigeons saved many lives with the messages they brought home. At the end of the war, those pigeons received medals for their bravery.

"As Sarge finished his history lesson, Ripley was fantasizing that he was one of those carrier pigeons flying over enemy trenches with soldiers trying to shoot him down. Up he went with the greatest of speed, artillery shells bursting all around him, now flying over the waters of the English Channel, dodging machine gunfire from enemy planes. When he made it home, all the pigeons were cheering him on, 'Hep-hep hooray! Hep-hep hooray!' The general from the Army was there to greet him. It was D who was pinning metal on his chest.

"Sarge noted Ripley was in another world, and he loudly called out Ripley's name. 'Do you mind sharing your thoughts with the rest of the class, Mr. Ripley?' All the young birds were looking at him, and in a low tone, he said no. Sarge looked directly at him and said,

'Well, I hope you got your metal.' Sandy hollered, 'Out, no! I did,' taking the attention off Ripley. Everyone burst out laughing, including Ripley. He was thankful for his sister for bailing him out. 'That's enough!' shouted Sarge. The classroom got quiet quick.

"'Thank you, Sarge,' said Rufus, 'for sharing that history lesson with us.' Sarge walked away. Rufus was in front of the class. 'Like I said before, there was three stock in our neighborhood. If you find yourself flying with strangers, you must separate yourself from them and come home when they start going down to their roof. You will also see pigeons like us. They have no coop, and they sleep out in the open. The trainers are calling them clinkers.'

"'Where do they get their food?' asked a youngster named Vicki.

"'Down in the street,' said Rufus. 'We fly above the roof. This stock flies hard, flies high, flies farther. Class dismissed. One more thing I have to say, we have a group of birds the trainers call the bombardiers. Some of your parents are members. All you need is endurance and plenty of it. When we are ripping away from home, we are mapping out our territory in all directions. I think some of you youngsters will find it exciting and adventurous. That's all for now.' Ripley told Sandy that he was going to join the bombardiers. 'So am I, slowpoke,' said Sandy. They couldn't wait to tell their parents the good news. The parents were proud to hear this. In order to be a leader, you must first be a bombardier later that evening.

"Farther up north, at Providence Rhode Island zoo, the exhibit hall is filled with smoke it's an electrical fire, and the Arabian Falcons ramses and Keziah are in a panic. Their next-door neighbors, two American Falcons, were down on the floor below the smoke line as the firemen hacked at the cages to set them free. When the sun came up, they found themselves huddled together on a branch of a big maple tree, looking down at the charred remains of the exhibit hall. The morning air had cleared their lungs, and they could smell again. Ramses told his mate, 'I smell warm air.' 'Yes, I smell it too. It's coming from the south,' she said. 'I'm hungry.' She lowered her head to take some silt off her three-inch toenails. This cold air did not suit them. They majestically lifted themselves forward into the air, and the two American falcons followed. Going through that howling experience together, a bond was formed. Up they went the firemen and workers waving at them, and one of them started singing 'Born Free.' They made many stops along the East Coast, now following the Hudson River heading toward New York City and stopping to hunt along the way.

"Birds Clyde and Rufus were waiting to drink from the water can. The door suddenly opened, and it was the super. He was coming to adjust the thermostat because the weather was getting warmer. Rufus asked Clyde, 'Do you smell that warm air coming through the open door?' Clyde told him, 'Soon, my friend, we'll be back on the roof. I can hardly wait to see the youngsters' reaction when we go up.' Something caught Rufus's eye. It was so fast he almost missed it. It was a creeper. 'Where?' asked Clyde, running into another room. Rufus said, 'There were a few rooms down in the basement. Tell everyone there's a creeper in the basement.'

"As the super was about to approach the door, he stopped and walked over to the pen, looking at them. 'You're lucky you're not chickens,' he said and then walked out and closed the door behind him. By this time, everybody knew it was going to be a long night, and the trainers wouldn't be back until tomorrow. It was deep into the night when the creeper came into view.

"Everyone had their eyes on him, and every bird was in their crate. Clyde studied him closely as he walked along the basement floor, trying to find a weakness in the screen. He poked and scratched, but there was no way in. He was a handsome fellow, all gray with a white streak that separated his eyes straight to his nose. He walked along the basement floor, pressing against the screen. The trainers anticipated this might happen.

"'The fellas did a good job in protecting us,' Clyde hollered at him. 'Go away, slow and deliberate.' He said, 'I am Mr. Gray, and this is my domain, and you sure look like chicken to me,' keeping his eyes on Clyde. Frustrated that he couldn't get in inside the holding pen, he just lay there with his tail going back and forth in a continuous movement, which actually made Clyde's eyelids heavy. All of a sudden, Mr. Gray was inside the pen, and he had Nova trapped with her two youngsters. As he slowly crept closer to them, Clyde was frozen with fear. He tried his best to get up, but he couldn't move. All he could do was watch the creeper.

"With his red tongue hanging out his mouth, he raised his ugly paw and struck Nova. Dizzy from the blow, she turned her body sideways with her left wing extended high over her head She snapped her right wing, slapping him across his nose. This infuriated Mr. Gray. He stood up on his hind legs with his front two paws showing his long claws, came down on them.

"Clyde hollered, 'No! No!' with the smack of Nova's wing and he woke up. He looked down to see if the creeper was still there, but he was gone. It was a bad dream. It was daylight now, and everyone was safe. Soon someone would come, and they hoped that they would notice the creeper was in the basement. No one dared to go down to eat or drink because of the creeper.

"The basement door slowly opened. It was D and with him his friend's dog, Peewee, who belonged to Carlos, D's friend. Carlos lived in the building on the top floor, and D would go to his apartment to fetch water for us during our stay on the roof. At first, Peewee used to chase us around, but D taught him how to sit and watch. If he wanted to hang out, he was brown all over. We liked him, as he was a good dog.

"D greeted us with 'What's up?' I noticed that everyone was in their crate and no one was feeding or drinking. To me that was strange. I looked down and noticed Peewee sniffing the basement floor and heading toward the other room, and all of sudden, a cat was running out, Peewee hot on his tail. He trapped the cat in a corner. I grabbed Peewee and held him back. I didn't want neither one of them to get hurt, holding Peewee by his collar. I walked to the door and opened it and walked to the back of the room with Peewee. The cat saw his opportunity to get away, and that was exactly what he did.

"I carefully examined the screen to see if there was any damage, and there was none. Peewee couldn't stand still, he was all over the place. He was making the birds nervous, so I decided to take him upstairs. Clyde was telling his family, 'God knows how long that cat would've been here with us if it wasn't for Peewee.' Sandy told her brother, 'Did you see that cat run? He sure had the tables turned on him. It serves him right for messing with our sleep,' as she leapt upward to the highest crate and perched herself there.

"Slowly and magically, a spider spun her way down to Sandy, and it spoke in a smooth melodic tone. 'Whatever you do, don't panic and don't let fear cloud your judgment and love with all your heart.' Then it proceeded to go back the way it came. With her head tilted, she kept an eye on the spider until it disappeared into the ceiling. She must've dozed off. D was walking inside the pen, and she didn't hear the basement door opening. *Was I dreaming?* she thought.

"I sat down on top of the water can, looking up at Sandy, perched on the top crate, urging her to come down as I padded my knee with my hand, now squeezing my lips together, making this annoying sound. 'Please stop, I'm coming.' Sandy jumped off, glided down for a few seconds, and pulled up flapping, landing on my knee. Nova looked down at Sandy and then D, started to sing to her. Nova noticed her daughter was blushing.

"Sandy remembered seeing those brown eyes peeking into the nesting bowl, as he said sweet things to her and her brother. Now she knew it was mostly for her, and she remembered the sweet smell of gum. 'Ripley, go get your sister. Can't you see that she's in love?' 'Nonsense,' said Nova. 'I'm only joking, Ma.' Ripley obeyed and landed on D's lap. It was more like a crash landing. D stopped singing and looked directly at Ripley, telling him they would be going up to the roof soon and to take care of his sister. 'Aye aye' Captain. 'You hear that, Sandy'.' He noticed a twinkle in his sister's brown eyes. As D started to rise up from the water can, they both flew up to their parents, Ripley teasing her all the way.

"Right before going down to the basement, looking down from the heavens was a goddess. Athena was her name, one of the many granddaughters of Zeus. The all-forgotten god of the sky, Zeus, sat on his throne on a floating castle made of clouds. Zeus heard his name being prayed to, which always caught his ear. When a mortal called out to him, he would say to himself, 'I am not forgotten.'

"So he sent his young granddaughter Athena to investigate this mortal, as she'd been mischievous lately, hoping this would keep her busy for a while. Her cousin Haytheus, who'd been waiting patiently for a mission, was disappointed. It Was D who said, 'Zeus, god of the sky, please bring my birds back to me,' remembering the movie *Hercules* when he was young. He repeated those words over and over again when the bombardiers were long overdue.

"Right away, Athena took an interest in these three young men and the way they cared for their birds. Her spiritual presence made these birds special, and the music coming out of the box was out' of this world. Her presence must have affected Sandy and Danny the most. She felt the love that D had for Sandy, which struck a sweet chord with her. If Athena concentrated hard enough, she could hear Sandy's prayers, which brought tears to her eyes and an overwhelming feeling of sadness. Zeus told her not to meddle in mortal affairs and to just observe. But she knows her grandfather always meddled in human affairs and changing their destiny. Now she was going to try her hand in changing Sandy's destiny. She's a romantic at heart. Athena decided to stick around until her masterpiece is completed. This caught the attention of a cousin Haytheus, who was jealous of her mission from the beginning. She felt his evil presence trying to sabotage her every move. The birds had really connected D to the heavens.

"Sandy was on the basement floor near the crate that was connected to the fence, and she heard a voice saying hello. It was a mouse. She wasn't frightened because she found him to be cute. He was cuter than the rats that she saw once in a while running along the wall. She said hello back, and asked, 'Where have you been hiding? What's your name?'

"'You can call me Mousy. I saw you talking to that spider. I've been trying to catch that crazy spider for a while now. What did she say to you?'

"'She told me not to panic and to love with all my heart.'

"'Will you help me catch her?' asked the mouse.

"'What has she done to you?' asked Sandy, and the mouse replied, 'She's a witch. You mustn't listen to her. She's evil, you must stay away from her.' He said it in a demanding manner.

"'It seems to me that you're the one that's evil,' said Sandy as she turned and flew up to her family.

"Not every bird has a mate, and not every egg hatches for reasons unknown. We'll be going up to the roof with twenty-one youngsters. We have over hundred birds."

CHAPTER 5

Up to the Roof We Go

As the days went by, it was an uneventful night until D turned off the light. We were in total darkness for the first time since our arrival. It was comforting not seeing anything and nothing seeing us. He lowered the volume on the radio. We knew he wanted us to have a peaceful night. Not a single peep from the youngsters, which was surprising; it had been about five months since we last saw the roof. Everyone went to sleep, dreaming about tomorrow. *Ticktock, ticktock.*

There was light coming through the basement window. The adults woke up to the noise the youngsters were making. Everyone was excited. Sarge hollered out, "Let's stretch those wings," which we did. The youngsters had been flapping around for at least a month now, taking up every inch of airspace. Once the basement was full of sunlight, the trainers came, all three of them. When Ray and Corky entered the pen, they started catching us, one by one, passing us to D. He was gently putting us in boxes, making sure the youngsters are with their parents. We were happy that we were leaving the basement and the creepers behind.

It was a bumpy ride up to the roof. Instantly we could smell the fresh air through the holes that the trainers made. Ray went inside the holding pen as the boxes were being passed to him. He tilted the boxes on its side, and we all slid out. It took a few seconds for our eyes to adjust to the bright sunlight. The youngsters were amazed at what they were seeing, feeling the heat from the sun for the first time. They were stunned by the beauty of the open sky. Most of the adults were perched on the two-by-four that stretched around the screen, looking down at the youngsters. Nova flew from where she was at straight into the coop to establish their sleeping quarters. Clyde followed, and he called out for Ripley and Sandy to come. Sandy and Ripley were right next door, and they flew back outside into the holding pen. All the adults had their eyes on the trainers, wondering what they were up to. The question the youngsters were asking was, "When are they going to let us out?'" The adults knew what the trainers were doing. They were letting the youngsters get acclimated to their new surroundings. Something caught the bird's attention, and the trainers turned their heads. It was the stock from Riverside Drive. The trainers were a little surprised to see them up so early in the morning. From this distance, everyone could see they were flying nice and tight. They looked good, hooking and swaying, and their tail-sitters did their thing.

The fellas were debating whether or not they should let the adults out first and keep the youngsters inside the screen a little longer. Then they finally came to the conclusion that the youngsters would stick by their parents. The birds, hearing Ray, said, "Let's do it now. Let's chase up, let's take advantage of the fact that choo-choo and Danny boy from a hunt Thirty-fifth and Stanley and his brother are sleeping. You tell them Ray!" shouted Sarge, and D and Corky were being cautious. They didn't want to lose any youngsters to those guys. But they agreed with Ray, who with confidence opened up all three trapdoors on the screen. I was looking at the open sky, and it was a little hazy, the sun hovering right over the horizon.

I looked around the roof and saw the water can was in its usual spot, the birds filtering out onto the roof floor. I saw Sandy and her brother. I wonder what they were thinking, adults leading the way being followed by the youngsters. Some of the adults flew to the edge of the roof, while the youngsters were flying all over the roof but no higher than the skylight. As we we're letting the youngsters take a good look at their roof, I noticed Sarge flying to the top of the coop followed by Rufus. Corky Ray and I were all leaning against the skylight wall. The door was to the right, and I hoped no one comes through the door. I got closer to the door just in case. We were being very quiet and still, making sure we didn't make any sudden movement. That would startled them into flight. As we were observing the youngsters' behavior, we were tickled pink. The day had finally arrived. Clyde's family flew to the top of the skylight, right over our heads. Perched higher than the birds on the roof, Ripley and Sandy could see a noisy train going by, seeing another one going in the opposite direction. Seagulls were flying over the river, and jersey it's all green. They see other roofs every one of them having a smokestack, to the left looking up, they saw the water tower made of bricks sitting on the project's roof. Some of the youngsters were on the edge of the roof, looking down on the street and watching the automobiles go up and down the avenue. Something caught the birds' attention high in the sky coming from Jersey. All of a sudden, all the youngsters were startled, frozen in their tracks by a sight that was not talked about in the basement.

A jet plane flew high over our heads, and quickly the adults had to explain to them, "It's not a bird of prey, and it's not even a bird. The iron bird comes and goes." Sandy looked at the iron bird as it flew away. "Where is that thing going to?" Sandy asked her father.

"It's going to land in Queens, which is straight ahead."

Sandy looked in that direction, seeing the iron bird getting smaller and smaller. Now she was looking at the park below with its green trees and the leaves moving with the wind. Now she felt the wind. *How mysterious*, she thought.

"I didn't realize how much I missed the sun," said Nova.

"The sun feels so good," said Sandy.

"It could also make you thirsty," said Clyde.

Ripley looked at the orange ball hanging in the sky and asked, "How did the sun get there, Dad?"

"I call it the master, the creator of what you're seeing, the sun. It's the giver of life."

Clyde heard Ray saying, "That's enough time on the roof. Let's do this."

Flying off the skylight, Clyde led his family to the edge of the roof. As Ray was walking toward the birds, Sarge rose up, flapping his wings, and up he went. They all followed and took off on their own, flying to the right, heading for the corner.

They circled the roof twice and came straight down. They looked like they were out of shape, which was a good thing for now, as they all landed on ledge, which was three feet in width and twenty-five feet in length.

That leaned out, which was the front of the building.

We had to take advantage of the fact that the two closest flyers were sleeping. We chased up a few times and then we let them rest and just lounge around the roof. We were confident when Stanley or his brother opens up, we be ready. Well, that time came, and Stanley was on the roof. He noticed that our birds were on the roof, so he hollered. "Welcome back! You got something for me?" I hollered back, "Remind us what it was."

"And if you do, I don't think so," he hollered back. He always had to get the last word. I don't understand Spanish. Stanley is cool; he makes me laugh.

Letting his birds out and feeding them, I remember telling Corky that Lucas was a tombola. I was waiting for him to tumble when our birds were flying. I named him Lucas, and it stuck. What he did in the basement was pretty amazing. I always name my favorite birds, and Lucas was one of them, even though he didn't belong to me.

I remember when Nova's eggs hatched, and I gave her two squabs their names. Ripley and Sandy—you can't go wrong with names like that, if you know what I mean, but I hit the hammer on the nail. I gave all my youngsters names, sometimes we called them by what they are—"Where's my young red Tiga?" And we all knew which birds he was talking about.

Stanley chased his birds off the roof. We knew sooner or later we would eventually have to chase up. Surely by now the youngsters knew this was their roof and that they belonged to it. Stanley's birds were now coming down and landing on his roof. Ray picked up the pole and chased up. The birds flew off the roof. Corky is whistling and clapping his hands and Ray screaming haah,

They took off to the right, and Stanley knew there were a bunch of youngsters in the stock. He immediately chased his birds right back up in the air, looking up at our birds flying straight and then a quick right turn and now a quick left turn.

And now circling over our roof—swaying, hooking, and swinging—Rufus and Sarge and Clyde were in control and purposely keeping a distance and not venturing into Stanley's territory. They were flying higher and higher, hooking and swaying. That was when Lucas started tumbling head over tail. He dropped out of a tight flying ball of birds straight down. He must've dropped fifty feet before he broke out of it and flew back up to continue flying with the birds.

It was one of the longest drop that I ever saw from a tombola. Stanley must've been amazed as we were. It was crazy. He did it only once, and then the stock from hundred and Thirty-Fifth Street was up and flying circles over there territory. Our birds avoided Stanley stock and were flying like they weren't there. Not a single youngster attempted to leave, which was a good thing. If you don't catch them now, you never will.

I knew the youngsters weren't going nowhere, not while their parents were flying for us. I had my eyes on Ripley and Sandy. The youngsters were flying like they had some kind of training. I was proud at what I was seeing, and I was sure that Ray and Corky had their eyes on their youngsters to.

Stanley kept trying to push his birds to make contact, but it just wasn't happening. Rufus, Clyde, and Sarge made sure that they had help the youngsters' mothers. As they came down, we slapped each other a high-five for a job well done.

It was late in the afternoon, and Ray had to go to work and Corky had to get ready for his dance classes. He was really talented. I remember when I visited his apartment seeing many trophies and pitches of his family winning awards. He came from a family of dancers, and they won many honors in many ballrooms throughout the city. He knows how to jitterbug. He was getting ready for the jitterbug contest at Madison Square Garden.

"Hold on a minute. Corky, why don't you show me and Ray how you dance the jitterbug?"

Athena was on the ledge with the birds, her legs dangling over the ledge. She was looking at the black flight with his white tips. He is beautiful, and she couldn't help but think what it would be like to have wings. Athena turned her head around, hearing our conversation.

"Come on, give us a demonstration," said Ray. "Corky, why are you hesitating? Don't tell us you're shy."

"How can I be shy when I'm going to be dancing in front of thousands of people? I need to dance with a partner for you guys to really appreciate it."

Ray told him, "Make believe you're dancing with one, okay?"

"Okay," he said and started acting like he had no energy. "Danny, find me some fast music." I turned the dial on the radio until I came upon the right song.

As soon as he heard the music, he burst into flames. Corky started to jitterbug, his arms extending out like he was holding some-one. Athena turned her body around, saying he needed a partner. Corky started dancing, his legs moving back and forth, now twirling the make-believe partner, who was now Athena. She followed Corky's lead as he grabbed her by her waist and twirled her behind his back. His index finger wiggled in the air, now holding the girl's left hand, and his right hand was behind her back. As they dipped and rocked back and forth, he really looked like he was dancing with someone. This was the first time Ray and I saw him dance the jitterbug. It was enjoyable to watch.

When the song finished, I said to Corky, "You're really good."

Ray asked, "Who's your partner?"

"Her name is Janel, and we meet three times a week for practice."

Athena was looking at Corky, clapping her hands. "That was so much fun. I'm gonna take that jitterbug with me." She was going to teach all her girlfriends how to jitterbug.

I turned the dial on the radio back to my station as the fellows walked toward the skylight. I was not going to chase up anymore, so I decided to clean out the coop of its poop. We always stayed on top of it. If you want healthy birds, it has to be done. After I dusted myself off, sat on the small brick wall, and watched them go about their own business. Sandy was perched on top of the pigeon coop, looking at me. The skylight door opened up it was Cassondra and Peewee. Sandy recognized her, as she came down to the basement a couple of times. She asked me if we lost any birds, and I told her no. She sat down next to me on the four-foot brick wall that separated the roofs. We talked, and I remember watching Peewee, hoping he wouldn't eat any of my birds. She called Peewee to come to sit next to her, and like a good dog, he obeyed.

I told her about Lucas tumbling, and she said she wished she could've seen that. I told her about the youngster that fell out his bowl, and Ray told me he found Lucas on the floor with a large bump on his head.

"Do you think he has brain damage from hitting the basement floor?"

"No, it's in his blood to tumble." Before I knew it, the sun was going down. That's when the birds wanted to go inside the coop. I asked Cassondra if she would help me lock up the birds, and with a smile, she said yes. I opened up all the trapdoors. She helped me maneuver the birds toward the coop. The adults knew what to do, and the youngsters followed, though some needed a little coaching. Sandy was the last one in.

I went inside the holding pen and put the metal plate against the opening of the pigeon coop, especially made with four holes one on each corner, which we brought at the metal shop. We had four large eyebolts sticking out the coop. I pushed the plate against the opening where the eyebolts would be sticking out and put the locks on them. I told the birds, "Good night, I'll see y'all tomorrow."

All the birds inside the coop said, "Good night, D."

Cassondra said, "You talk to them? I hope you're not expecting them to answer you back."

All the flyers in the hood were doing the same thing. I walked her and Peewee down to her apartment and headed home. I couldn't wait to come back.

Inside the coop, there was a buzz in the air, and all the youngsters were talking about the open sky and how beautiful the world is and that it belongs to them. They were now bragging about what they did and how wonderful it felt flying altogether at the same time. They were coming to terms with why the trainers would chase them off the roof and realized that was part of the relationship between them. It had been the way since man and pigeons became partners. They mean no harm. Some of the birds asked, "Lucas, how did you do that?"

Some of the youngsters were lowering their heads as Lucas walked by. His reply was, "It's in the blood. Either you have it or you don't," and strutted away.

Ripley and Sandy were perched in their cubbyhole above, looking down. Ripley said to Sandy, "Who made him prince?"

Sandy replied, "That was impressive."

"What was?" said Ripley.

"Are you jealous?"

"No," Ripley replied quickly.

Sandy said to her brother, "You'll always be my prince," as she bowed her head.

Ripley put his wing on top of Sandy's head and said, "From this day forth, you shall be my obedient servant," stopping Sandy from rising.

Sandy hollered, "Mom! Ripley is bothering me."

Nova hollered back, "Stop it, Ripley, or I'm going to tell your father when he gets back."

Ripley removed his wing, and Sandy said, "A fine king you will make."

Clyde was down below talking to Sarge and Rufus about how good it felt to be free again. "Let's see what tomorrow brings," said Sarge. "Every day we must fly a little longer, a little higher, a little farther so we could be the best stock in the hood and make our trainers happy." Clyde and Rufus agreed. Clyde said good night to his friends and flew back up to his cubbyhole.

Nova was waiting there, and he lay down beside her, giving her a loving poke on the head. She asked, "Do you think Ripley will find his niche?"

"Sure he will," said Clyde. "They all will."

"Did you see what Lucas did?" said Nova.

"Yes," said Clyde. "He has made a big impression on the youngsters. They're all looking up to him."

Nova said, "He needs to be more careful when he's tumbling. He may get dizzy and pass out."

"But I'm sure his parents are talking to him right now," said Clyde.

Sandy and Ripley came closer and asked their parents, "How did we do?"

Clyde said, "You both made us proud."

Later that night, Sandy perched on the empty cubbyhole next to the vent, which was four inches long and four inches wide, looking at the stars and questioning her feelings for D. He is a human being, and I was born a pigeon. Why does my heart want to jump out of my chest every time I see him? She heard music, and tears flooded her brown eyes. She could clearly hear the words, "I'm wishing on a star, to follow where you are, I'm wishing on a dream, to follow what it means, I'm wishing on a star.[1]" Why did I have to be born a pigeon? she thought as she silently cried herself to sleep.

---

[1]   Wishing on a star by, Rose Royce.

CHAPTER 6

Hi-ho Silver

Clyde looked around as everyone was falling asleep. He was thinking, what an exciting day. Clyde was sure D would be opening up as the sun hit the horizon. As he was thinking that, he also fell asleep. As daylight began to shine through the air vent, Sandy woke up from a beautiful dream she was having and told her brother. Its a brand-new day.

"Mom, Dad, wake up. I'm hungry," Ripley squawked.

"Soon, my son. When D opens up, we're all going to chow down."

*****

I practically ran up the block. I stopped by the basement and picked up the radio and headed up to the roof.

*****

Everyone felt the vibration on the roof floor as someone was coming close. They heard the screen door opening and the locks on the metal plate being opened with their distinctive clicks. As the metal plate was being removed, all the youngsters rushed out into the holding pen. It was a beautiful morning, and the sun was hanging right over the edge of the roof. He kept us in the holding pen as we watched him messing around with the radio. When he was finished doing that, he picked up the water can and headed down to get some fresh water. When he came back, he came over and said "good morning" to everyone while he was opening up the trapdoors to let us out.

*****

I placed a big pan of food on the roof floor. The night before, I crushed a vitamin pill into a fine powder and sprinkled some of it over their food, and I sat down and started watching them. After they finish eating, I noticed there was a long line at the water can.

*****

Rufus told Sarge, "Who changed the menu? Whatever it is, you know it's good for us."

*****

I was in no rush to chase them up. There'd be plenty of time for that. I turned on the radio. It was connected by a long cord leading into the skylight. There was a lot of groovy dancing going on, and the males were strutting their stuff, trying to impress the females.

I saw Ripley had two left feet, and he kept tripping over them. I shouldn't laugh. I'm not a very good dancer myself. As always, Sandy was on top of the coop looking at me, and I was staring right back at her. I was supposed to be looking uptown to see if any pigeon coop was open, but no, I was playing silly games with Sandy. I loved this bird. I walked up to her and got real close. She didn't flinch. I put my face right in front of hers, looking into her eyes. She didn't move, so I softly blew my breath in her face. She closed her eyelids. I turned around, and not a single stock was flying.

I took a quick look toward the east side—they were miles away. From the front of the roof looking straight ahead toward Queens, you could almost see the jetliners going down to land at LaGuardia Airport. Sometimes the direction of the wind wasn't right, and they would fly right over us. It was so quiet on the roof, except for my music. You forget there are people down in the street going about their business.

My birds connected me to the heavens, and there was nothing but open skies as far as the eye could see. I thought maybe that's why when the birds are ripping they never lose sight of home, and being on top of the hill didn't hurt either. While I was looking in that direction. I saw a bird streaking through the sky at a high rate of speed right across the horizon, flying in a straight line. I figured it was a homing pigeon going home.

One of my favorite songs was about to come on. I pushed the birds to the ledge of the roof and picked up the bamboo pole, which we got from the pet shop, and used it as an extension of my hand so that I would never lean over the roof.

And off they went. They sure seemed to be in a hurry, making a right turn at the corner and now coming back flying above my head. I see Sandy and Ripley right behind the leaders, and they were heading into Stanley's territory, hooking and swaying high over Stanley's roof. Slowly drifting back, Sandy looked down on Stanley's roof and saw the pigeon coop and its holding pen—no birds. Following the rhythm of the stock, Sandy looked down and saw D looking up.

I was watching them, and they looked like waves at the beach coming from the left in layers and landing on the landing pad as the music played. I was thrilled with their performance. Looking up, I saw that same bird—I could tell by the way it was flying with the same urgency as before. First flying uptown, now flying downtown, flying very fast, it appeared to be all white. I started poking the birds.

Patty asked, "What's poking?"

"Well, poking is using the long bamboo stick to chase a few birds from the landing pad to the top of the coop, back and forth, trying to get the attention of the lost bird above to let it know there's a pigeon house on this roof. Where was I... Oh, the pigeon must have seen the stock flying and made a U-turn back this way. It was either a flight or tiplet. Whatever it was, it was fast and it flew past Knickerbocker Hospital and kept going straight downtown. I lost sight of it. I sat down on the wall and started looking at Sandy on the landing pad. She was looking back at me, and I was blowing kisses at her. Something caught my eye, and it was that bird again but much closer this time.

"I could see it clearly it was all white and it was fast, and I mean *fast*. I could tell this bird was in distress by the speed it was using, desperately trying to find its home. This bird was definitely lost. I picked up the pole and chased up the birds that were on the landing pad and left the rest of them on the roof floor as the flying birds were making that turn at the corner. The stray was coming into our territory. I have seen this before… I got it! *The Lone Ranger*. I loved *The Lone Ranger* when I was a kid. This was my chance to catch me a white stallion. We had all different colored birds, except a solid white one. This would be a feather in my cap.

"The birds were now flying high above the project, circling. I wanted this white bird, so I picked up the pole and maneuvered the rest of the birds up to the ledge. Looking up, I saw it flying around the stock. I needed my birds to consume it and bring it down."

*****

Ripley was among the birds that were flying. Noticing the bird above him, he went up to greet her. "It's a beautiful day for flying, isn't it?" Ripley asked charmingly.

"I'm lost. I don't know which way to go."

"You're not lost," said Ripley. "You just found yourself a new home. Why don't you come down with us and have something to eat and drink, and if you don't like it here, you can leave. I'll guide you down."

*****

Looking up, the white stallion was about to join the stock. I didn't want to take any chances, so I chased up the rest of the birds. Now I have two small stocks in the air flying. I took a quick look up town to see if any stock were in the air. I was happy to see that they were all still sleeping.

With no competition, I should be able to bring this bird down. It was still flying circles around the stock as both stocks became one. She seemed to settle down a little bit. As the birds were descending, she was outside the stock tagging along. I walked to the skylight wall, standing still. I watched this bird trying to make up its mind. As the birds were landing, she was the last one to touch down. The second half of the game was about to start.

I was looking at this bird, and it was dynamically perfect. It was one of the most beautiful birds I'd ever seen. It was born to cut through the wind and had boot feathers running down her leg. This was one good-looking bird. Now I was excited I walked slowly toward the screen and picked up the string that connected the trapdoor at the bottom. I grabbed a handful of feed and started to throw some toward the trapdoor, but she wasn't biting; she was looking at the water can. Slowly I moved it a bit closer to her and then backed away. If she dipped her head to drink, that would be the perfect time to grab her. She wouldn't see me coming.

She saw the other birds drinking and she flew onto the roof floor, hesitating, all the way to the water can. The more she saw the other birds drinking, the more she wanted to drink. She was thirsty, all right. And when she reached the water can and dipped her head to drink, I grabbed her.

Rufus hollered, "Were your youngsters paying attention?"

As I'm holding the white tiplit in my hands, I'm getting goose bumps. Someone lost a beautiful bird, I thought to myself. *She belongs to me now!* I get to put my yellow band on her leg and she belongs to the yellow clang I was so excited I couldn't wait for Corky or Ray to come up so I could show her off. They had never caught anything as beautiful as this white tiplet, and she was young. I put her inside the screen and closed the door. A couple of days inside the coop, she would know this was her new home and bond with the birds.

I was standing with my hands on top of the screen, checking out my new bird, I remember Sandy flying up to the top of the screen. I looked up as she was coming toward me. She plucked me with her beak on my hand. I told her, "Don't get jealous. You know

I love you," as she sat there looking at me. I couldn't take my eyes off her, like I was hypnotized.

Ripley flew to the floor next to the scream and started a conversation with the new bird. He asked her what her name and she replied, "Snowflake. Do you have anything funny to say about my name?"

"Other than the fact, I never would've guessed."

"What's yours?"

"Ripley."

"Nice name," she said. "Is your trainer good?" she asked with curiosity.

"The best," he said, "all three of them. They're all good to us, which is really important. If we're not happy, we couldn't be the best stock in the hood. Down in the basement, D was nominated number one, but we didn't tell the other two. We don't want to hurt their feelings. My sister is up there now, trying to get his attention."

"That's not normal," said Snowflake.

"My mother said she'll grow out of it. I know you'll like it here. I guarantee it."

"How long will I be locked up?" asked Snowflake.

Ripley replied, "Just a couple of days. This way you get to know everyone. Just relax, everything will be fine. Soon you be out here flying with us and having fun. I'm glad you decided to stay."

"I don't think I had a choice. I would never drink out of a water can again," Snowflake said with a shutter, and Ripley laughed.

*****

I heard my name being called, and it was Cassondra, walking toward the back. The smell of breakfast was all over the roof rising from the windows down below. Looking down at the alley, I saw Cassondra's face sticking out the window, and she asked me if I wanted some breakfast and to come down and join them. I told her I'd be right down. The first thing I did was grab my beautiful bird and put her inside the coop just in case someone comes up and she wouldn't be an easy pick.

*****

Sarge and Rufus were on top of the screen as usual, watching the youngsters at play. One of the youngsters named Charlie was sneaking off. He was at the back of the coop on the ledge, walking toward the back of the roof. Charlie looked down at the alleyway; he was hearing Jamaican music for the first time. Nothing like that was being played on the radio down in the basement. It was coming from a window down below, the music seemed to fill him up with joy. The birds at the front of the roof also heard it. Charlie danced to the rhythm and, as he got closer, leapt off the ledge right across from Cassondra's window to the fourth floor, landing on the edge of the window. On top of the screen, Sarge was telling Rufus that our adversaries, the nomads, were on their roof being let out.

*****

In the apartment, as I was helping wash the dishes, I heard my name being called. It was Ray, and he was on the roof. I stuck my head out the living room window and told him I had a surprise for him and that I'd be right up. In a flash, I came through the skylight door onto the roof, and he asked, "Where is the surprise?"

I told him, "I caught a fantastic-looking tiplet this morning." I walked into the screen and unlocked the plate door and stepped out and waited for the tiplet to step out. When she did, I heard Ray say, "That's one beautiful tiplit." Ray looked her over and told me, "It looks like a show bird."

"Not the way she was flying. Show birds are prized for their beauty, and they come in all colors. They are picked for their perfect features, not for their flying skills." He asked me when I caught her, and I said, "Early this morning. You should've seen the way she was flying."

"How did you catch it?"

"When she went to drink some water, that's when I grabbed her."

Ray said, "My man," and gave me a high-five. Jerry and Stanley's birds were on the roof. I turned around to look, and we didn't see anyone up there, so Ray thought it was safe. He picked up the pole and chased up. Those sneaky guys were hiding, waiting for us to chase our birds up. We saw them running to the front of the roof, chasing up.

Both stocks kept their distance from each other, circling over their roof, and once the birds reached a certain height, there were no boundaries; the sky belongs to everyone. Some of the bombardiers were starting to rip away from the stock. About eight of them were heading across town. As our stock circled high above, we tracked the bombardiers flying across city college, now across Saint Nicholas Park, Dutchman's territory. Passing music and arts high school, they continued going uptown. I knew Jerry and Stanley were hoping this would be the day that both stock would clash, hoping to steal away some youngsters from us. We were not looking forward to that, but if it happens, we would deal with it. As our stock was flying, we noticed the youngsters were no longer trailing behind. They were flying nice and tight, hooking and swaying. We preferred a small stock. It was organized flying, nice and tight, and they stayed up in the air longer. Now in a big stock, say, about two hundred birds, the birds flying down below tend to keep the birds above from going any higher.

Stanley was on top of his coop, waving at us. His birds were coming down, and so was ours. As our birds were hitting the roof, Ray was looking at our birds to see who was missing. He started naming them Sarge, Rufus, and Clyde. I didn't see Ripley and Sandy, Lucas, Bingo, and Penny. I sat down on the wall, and we waited. Ray told me, "Don't worry. Sarge will bring them back."

I said, "I know he will."

Scanning the sky, the birds from Riverside were up and flying. We noticed Danny boy from 135th Street was open for business. His birds were going up, and we suddenly realized it was our eight birds that were coming back flying high over their territory. Our birds were coming home like homers straight toward us, flying above Danny boy's birds. Our eight birds started to descend, and they were about to pass Jerry and Stanley's roof when Lucas decided to tumble. Their birds were underneath, and Lucas started to celebrate too soon, stumbling down right into a flying hornet's nest. Lucas tried to get away but couldn't maneuver his way out. Jerry's birds blocked his every move. Ray immediately chased our birds up, hitting the corner and now coming back over our heads. We were hoping that Lucas would notice that he was flying with the wrong stock.

As the ripping birds joined our stock up above, Sarge noticed what was happening, but he did not want to engage. Instead, he watched over the rest of the youngsters, who would be in more danger of getting caught by our adversaries. Lucas was on his own, and he was caught in their web when their birds went down.

They knew of Lucas's exploits, and he would be one prized possession if only they could catch him. He was one of a kind. Ray and I were anxious, looking at their birds landing on their roof. That's one bird I didn't want to lose to them, plus Corky wouldn't be too happy his favorite bird being caught. Lucas was forced to land on a strange roof, and we were watching to see their next move. The first thing Lucas noticed was that the trainers did not look like his and that it was not his pigeon house. Suddenly he realized no one was stopping him from leaving, so without hesitation, he took off from their roof. Before they could set a trap for him, flying with all his might, he came straight to our roof.

When Lucas landed on the roof, Ray and I looked at each other with a sigh of relief. "I had a few tumblers in the past," Ray said, "and seen many of good tumblers, but I have never seen anything like Lucas. I think the fall he had might've messed him up a little bit. I think he's a little crazy."

"Well, he can't be that crazy," I said. "He knew he was on the wrong roof. I think he's pretty smart."

Ray said, "There's something weird about his tumbling. He seems to fall asleep."

I turned away from Ray, looking for Lucas, and hollered at him, "Are you falling asleep on the job, Mr. Lucas?"

Lucas hollered back, "No, sir, I don't think so, sir."

"You better not." Ray looked at me and said, "You're the one that's crazy."

We chased up a few times, and I had my eyes on Lucas. Later that day, Corky came up, and we told him what happened to Lucas and, of course, the bird that I caught. He walked over to the holding pen. "She's beautiful. She'll make a nice addition to the stock." We sat and chatted. We told him about the birds ripping like they did last summer. He spoke about his jitterbug classes, and Ray wished he had more time with the birds, but he had to learn the business because his mother was planning to buy him the store.

Little Joe asked, "Did you catch any strays that day?"

"I don't remember. We caught a lot of strays that summer. Sometimes the people who fly birds will take they strays to the pet shop and trade them in for cash or food. We were fortunate enough to have Ray flying with us. He had a steady income, while I was still on allowances. I could've gotten a summer job, but I wanted to be on the roof with the birds. Sometimes young beginners would come up to our roof to buy some birds, and we would sell them the strays that we thought they could stick."

"Because we remember our humble beginnings to stick," said Patty.

I told her, "I would sell them birds that will most likely stay with them. Hence the word *stick*, to stick around. Ray made sure that we didn't need anything. The last time we went to the pet shop, we noticed a bag on the counter that looked like grits but pink. We asked Mike, 'What is that?' He told us, 'That's pink grits. It will help your birds digest their food more efficiently.'

"Birds will sometimes swallow little rocks to help grind their food. Ray took some money out of his pocket and bought a two-pound bag of the pink grits. Maybe that's why our birds seemed to have more energy than any of the stock in our neighborhood. We had the best-looking bird and the healthiest. We would put a pan full of water on the roof so they could bathe, and then they would lie down and sunbathe on the roof with their wings stretched out like they were on the beach. As I was watching them, an elderly Puerto Rican woman came up from the next roof, asking me to sell her a bird. I thought she was looking for a pet. I asked her why, and she replied in Spanish that she wanted to make pigeon soup. I told her, 'I'm sorry I can't,' and she said, 'But you have so many.' She asked why, and I told her I love my birds.

One of the kids said, "Pigeon soup!"

Later that day, we were always trying something new to make us better. It was going to be a warm night with a full moon. We agreed to keep this to ourselves. As time went by, Ray eventually had to go to work. Corky and I stood on the roof with the birds until the sun went down. I agreed to take the first watch since I was having dinner at Carlos's house. I liked Cassondra, and I think she liked me too. Their mother was making my favorite dishes, chicken and dumplings. I told the fellas I would check on them periodically to make sure no one would steal our birds. Ray said he got off at twelve and that he'd come up and check on them. Corky said he'd come up with Ray, which they did, and we stood over in Carlos's apartment to about one thirty that night. No one knew the birds were sleeping on the roof. The roof was even quieter at night.

CHAPTER 7

A Bad Moon Is Rising

Most of the birds were congregating around the screen, waiting to get inside the coop, but no one was opening up the doors. Sarge, Clyde, and Rufus were on top of the screen, trying to figure out what was going on. There was a lot of chatter coming from the birds on the roof floor. Sarge walked up to the ledge of the holding pen and addressed the birds below, "We're spending the night on the roof. The trainers did not forget about us. They're doing this purposely."

"Why?" one of the birds hollered from below.

"They are bonding us to the roof," said Sarge. Clyde and Rufus were by his side now.

"We're already bonded to this roof," said Rufus.

"They want us to feel that the roof is our home," said Sarge.

"That doesn't make any sense," said Clyde.

"It does to them," said Sarge. "They are in command."

"I thought you were, Sarge. All this time, I've been talking to the wrong pigeon," Rufus said, poking fun at Sarge.

Clyde turned to the crowd below. "Let's all just relax and enjoy the night air. We don't get to see the stars often, so this is one for the books." Rufus said, who was the keeper of the book with recorded history of the stocks. Every bird's name is in it, with events, defeats, and triumph, as well as the names of lost friends and new ones. So the birds down below started to disperse, going in different directions and finding a comfortable place to sleep.

They did have some light coming from the moon and light rising up from the streets below. Some of them remained on the landing pad and on the roof floor, while some on top of the holding pen on the plywood that covered the top. Realizing that there would be some sleeping on top of the roof tonight, they made the best of it. Some huddled together and some in private little corners. This wasn't too bad, they thought, compared to the night that D turned off the light in the basement. Sandy and her family were on top of the holding pen. It had been a long day, and it felt good to sleep under the moon and the stars for a change.

D came up a couple of times, waking everybody up, checking up on us, and making sure no one was on the roof.

"The moon is overhead," Nova said to Clyde as they cuddled together. "Isn't this romantic? The moon is staring at us."

Sandy giggled at her parents, and Ripley told her to shut up. Then sleep and peace fell over the stock.

*****

Someone was watching. Down in the alley, the cats were gathering as one of the scouts reported to Mr. Gray. A little winded from running down the stairs, he approached Mr. Gray, telling him, "There are birds on the roof."

"Tell me something I don't know."

"There are birds on the roof," repeated the scout.

Mr. Gray got in the face of the scout, with his lips curled, showing his fangs and raising his paw seconds away from slapping Knuckles silly. Mr. Gray paused. "Did you say there are birds on the roof?"

"Yes, yes, they're not inside the coop. There are birds all over the roof," said Knuckles.

Mr. Gray turned his head, looking up between the clothesline that connected the buildings. "Yes, I see them," he said with an evil grin. Turning to the scout, he said, "Why didn't you say so?" Then he told him to get the rest of the gang and that they could stop foraging. "We found our meal for tonight."

Gray walked the alley between two buildings. It was quiet passing row of empty garbage cans, just like his stomach. Looking at the two sets of stairs, he chose the one to the right, one roof over. On top of the stairs, a dim lightbulb was lit over the door. Mr. Gray walked up the metal stairs to the top, and he turned around, whipping his claws out. At the edge of the step, he sharpened his claws. Coming into view between the two buildings were some of the meanest cats in the neighborhood, climbing over barriers and coming toward him. Joining him was Geronimo and Caesar and Knuckles, the scouts.

They were on top of the stairs now, looking at Mr. Gray and waiting for his command. "Let's go," he said, leading the way through the open door and turning toward the stairs that led to the roof. It was quiet, and everybody was sleeping. As they marched up, they noticed that every landing had a window and that the moon was shining through all the windows. They followed Mr. Gray in a single file, and as they reached the fourth floor, little did they know on the opposite window Peewee was lying on the sofa chair dreaming about Thanksgiving.

*****

Hearing a voice in his ear telling him to wake up, Peewee slowly opened his eyes. Looking straight toward the living room window, he saw cats creeping up the stairs through the window of the stairwell the building over. Peewee jumped off the sofa chair and ran to the window. He knew where they were going—up to the roof. He heard D tell Cassondra earlier this evening that the birds were going to spend the night on the roof. He turned around and ran, turning the corner and into Cassondra's bedroom, and jumped on the bed and started barking. Upset and confused, Cassondra woke up and decided to check on the apartment and get a drink of water. Everything seemed fine. On her way to her bedroom, she noticed Peewee scratching at the front door.

Meanwhile, on the roof, Mr. Gray and his boys were at the skylight door one roof over, formulating a plan of attack. They decided to attack from three different directions. The cat named Geronimo would walk on the front ledge of the roof and jump up to the next roof, and Caesar would walk the ledge that led to the back of the coop. Mr. Gray and the scout would go up the middle and jump on the wall that the trainers sat on.

*****

Clyde woke up to a familiar but muffled sound but then fell back to sleep.

*****

The cats began to execute their plan with their good night vision, which allowed them to see everything—pigeons on the ledge, pigeons on the floor, and pigeons on top of the holding pen. Studying the situation, they decided to grab and snatch. But Geronimo jumped the gun, creeping along the ledge and trying to get closer to a bunch of sleeping birds. He leaped and grabbed one. Upon seeing this, Mr. Gray jumped into a bunch of birds on the floor. The scout hesitated. The birds on top of the holding pen were startled by what was happening, and they could see an outline of a cat on the ledge of the roof with the help of the light coming from the street. Before they knew it, there was a cat on top of them. All of a sudden, the door from the skylight opened, and the light from the bulb gave them a couple of seconds of clarity, trying to fly away from danger. They realized it was Peewee coming to the rescue. Geronimo had a bird by his wings, and it slipped away. And the cat on top of the coop, well, there was nothing to be had. The birds were now up in the air, flying. Thank God for the full moon.

Mr. Gray noticed Peewee approaching, and he started hissing and spitting at Peewee, not wanting to let go of the bird he had. He stood his ground, holding down a bird named Red with one paw, and with the other he whipped out his knives. Peewee, with a low growl, showed his pearly whites. The cat on top of the pigeon coop threatened to leap, and the scout that was on the brick wall was hissing and spitting, arching his back, trying to make himself look bigger.

Peewee did not hesitate and jumped Mr. Gray, who instantly let go of the bird he had in his grip. He scratched Peewee on the side of his face, but Peewee dodged left and right and bit Mr. Gray on the butt.

Seeing Mr. Gray jump over the wall, the other cat scurried behind him as Peewee balked at them as they ran through the skylight door and disappeared into the night.

Pee Wee walked back to the skylight, opened up the door, and sat down, holding the door open, so the light from the skylight could shine on the pigeon coop. The birds could see it was safe to land again, except for a few missing feathers.

No one was lost—one for the book.

*****

I woke up anxious, got dressed, and went straight up to the roof. There I was met by Peewee and I took a quick look at the birds at the landing pad. They seemed calm enough. Peewee came over to say hello. I looked over the birds and I saw Sandy and Ripley; no one was missing. I noticed pigeon feathers floating along the roof floor, not little ones but large red feathers, the ones that are attached to the wings. I heard the skylight door opening behind me. It was Ray, and I brought it to his attention.

"Do you think Peewee was messing with the birds?" he asked.

"I don't know," I replied. I walked around to the front of the holding pen, close to the wall. Looking down, I noticed some more feathers and some red spots that looked like blood on the roof floor. I followed the trail of blood, which led to the other roof and straight into the skylight and down the stairs. I went no farther. Walking back, I hoisted myself up to our roof.

Ray said, "What did you find, Sherlock Holmes?"

"Cats," I told him. I called Peewee to come to me, and when he did, I started patting him on his head, telling him he was a good dog. His tail kept whipping back and forth.

I told Ray it was probably that gray cat, and right away Peewee gave out a bark. Then we started wondering which bird lost its feathers. We narrowed it down to six birds. I told Ray we would probably be able to tell which bird was attacked when they be flying.

"I was thinking the same thing," said Ray.

I picked up the water can and went down with Peewee to get some clean water. On my way down, Corky was on his way up and he asked, "Is everything okay?" I could see that concerned look on his face.

"The birds had a visitor last night."

"Who?"

"It was a cat. I also found Peewee on the roof."

"What was he doing up there?"

"I don't know," I said. "But I'm glad he was. Carlos, who answered the door, had this puzzled look on his face when he saw Peewee."

Snowflake slept right through all the commotion. She felt comfortable in her new pigeon house. Outside the birds were talking about last night, and thanks to Peewee, they did manage to get some sleep. It was a beautiful day, and Sarge told Rufus and Clyde to tell the rest of the birds to forget about last night and to do some flying and save the stories for their grandkids.

Corky was telling Ray, "Now that we nightstick them, we shouldn't lose a single bird." I heard him say that as I walked onto the roof with fresh water in the water can. We took a big chance in doing that, but I guess it was worth it, knowing that the birds were bonded not only to the coop but also the roof.

It was early seven o'clock to be exact. We were always the first to open up because "the early bird catches the worm." No one bothered to take the plate off the coop, being that all the birds were already on the roof. I took the plate off to let Snowflake out into the holding pen. When she came out, she had Ray and Corky's attention.

Corky asked me, "When are you going to let her out?"

"Maybe tomorrow," I answered. No one had eaten breakfast, so I asked the fellas if they wanted a scrambling eggs sandwich. Of course, they said yes. "Breakfast is cheap, fellas." I put out my hand, and they both donated a dollar. As I turned to go, Ray shouted, "With bacon."

"Don't push your luck," I said.

I heard Ray saying, "Stray at ten o'clock," as I was walking down the stairs. I heard them chasing the birds up. Inside the apartment, I gave Cassondra three dollars, and she asked, "What's this for?"

"Some scrambled eggs for me and the fellas," I replied. She tried to give it back, but I wouldn't take it. I told her I found Peewee on the roof.

"Please tell me he didn't do anything to your birds."

"No, everything is fine," I told her. She told me she let him out last night, thinking he had to do his business, and as she waited for him, she fell back asleep.

I came up with the sandwiches and asked Ray, "Where's the stray?"

"It flew away," said Ray.

"The birds are flying overhead. We know which bird was mauled by the cat," said Corky. "It's Ray's red flight."

Ray pointed up to his red flight. You could see he was trying his best to keep up with the stock. We could see the gaps between his feathers on his left wing. As the stock flew over the water tower, the red flight dropped out and landed on top of the water tower and bank there. The rest of the stock continued flying.

Lucas was tumbling and flying back up to join the stock, and as they started to descend, as I approached the holding pen looking at my beautiful white tiplit, I wondered where she came from, knowing someone was on the roof crying about losing this bird. She flew up to the two-by-four, looking at the birds on the roof, and she looked content. She leapt into the air in the middle of the holding pen, flapping her wings and hovering. She returned to the two-by-four, and I had this wonderful feeling about this bird. She was white as snow, and I thought I should call her Snowflake.

I took my eyes off her and watched the birds touching down on the landing pad and then looked at Ray and Corky. I decided I was going to add a little excitement to our day by letting her out while all the flyers in the hood were sleeping. I knew I only had her for one day and, in a low tone, I asked her if she was going to stay if I let her out. Ray heard me talking and said, "It's too early to let that white tiplet out. You should at least keep it in for two more days. It's too pretty to lose."

"She's going to stay, Ray, believe me," I said.

"How do you know it's a she?" he asked.

I replied, a bird that pretty, has to be a girl. Okay, it's a girl, said ray, but you only had her in the coop for one day, hearing Corky, saying you better listen to Ray, I said all the flyers are still sleeping, you taking a big chance said Corky, believe me I said she landed on this roof because she wanted to, she's already stuck, 'shaking their heads and Corky said, you're going to get burned dude.

I opened up the screen door so she could walk out, and she stood on the roof floor looking at me and then turned to look at Ray. Then she flew up to the ledge with the rest of the birds. She started flapping away, hovering three feet off the roof and then coming down. She did this a few times. "She looked like she's ready to take off," said Ray, and before he could finish, she took off straight ahead toward the open sky.

Seeing her flying away from us, maybe I should've listened. I immediately chased the birds off the roof, and they took off, diving down for momentum and reaching the corner. Gaining altitude, they were now flying straight up high over our heads. Ripley had his eyes on Snowflake as she flew farther away. He wanted to go after her, but he didn't want to break formation.

I heard Corky saying, "I should've listened to them. Baby, don't let me down." I had my fingers crossed and then I noticed that she was making a U-turn, back toward us. Cutting through the wind, she caught up with the stock, which divided itself in half. The top stock then disappeared behind the project with Snowflake.

I lost sight of the top stock for a few minutes, and then it reappeared, flying over Corky's building and Knickerbocker Hospital. They made a left going uptown, flying the length of St. Nicholas Park, and we watched them streaking across the horizon like homing pigeons, while the other half was flying over our roof, hooking and swaying.

CHAPTER 8

Joe the Crow

As the red flight sat on the water tower, he didn't notice that a crow landed behind him. The crow noticed the bird and started walking toward him. "Are you okay?" asked the crow.

"Why do you ask?" replied the red flight.

"Because you pigeons usually fly away from us."

"We were attacked last night by gangs of cats, Mr. Gray and his boys." The red flight could feel his wing swelling up. He was in too much pain to fly away.

The crow said, "You have something else to fear."

"You," said the red flight, feeling a little uncomfortable.

"Falcons," said the crow. "There's a family of falcons across the waters. If you look hard enough, you can see them hovering over the trees."

The red flight was listening and looking over to Jersey, and he saw them. There was a crow next to the red flight on the water tower. "That's interesting. I wonder what's going on."

*****

I turned my head and noticed the ripping birds were returning. Snowflake was among them, and you couldn't help but notice her.

Corky told Ray, "That crow is gonna jump your flight. He knows it's wounded."

"The flight is too big," said Ray. The ripping birds joined the bottom stock. Ray told me I was lucky.

"I knew she was gonna stay," I replied. "It's her destiny to fly with the best stock in the neighborhood."

The birds descended upon the roof, and we could finally relax. We talked among ourselves, and the birds were relaxing from their journey.

Sarge asked Clyde, "Did you see all those birds of prey across the waters?"

"Yes," said Clyde.

"They all the way over there and we're safe here, but there's a lot more than I remembered," said Sarge with a slight quiver in his voice.

"Don't worry, Sarge. They hardly ever cross the river," Clyde said with his mouth full of food. "Now eat something, Sarge. Stop worrying and let's just hope they stay on their side."

*****

It was another beautiful day with very few clouds. Time was passing by, and I looked over the roof and saw some of my friends playing basketball in the schoolyard. I decided I was going down to join them, and Corky decided to tag along. Ray decided to stay with the birds. He preferred watching over chasing, unless he sees a stray. He was good at catching strays.

Ray noticed a brown bag on top of the coop; he forgot he brought his binoculars. He took them out of the bag. They were real helpful last summer watching the birds rip and "hitting pins"—the terminology for when your birds fly so high they look like the head of pins.

Stanley and Jerry were our adversaries. Across the way, Ray noticed their birds were flying and that one bird in particular was not flying in harmony with the rest of the stock. Ray figured it was a new bird, and he chased our birds up, hoping to pull the new bird into our territory and catch him. When there's a stray in the air. We compete for that stray. There is a strong competition among us to see who's the best at catching strays.

Jerry's birds were coming down, and that bird was going down with them. Our birds were flying high now, and Ray focused back on his birds. Then he noticed some birds were ripping away from the stock and that they were headed uptown.

When the flyers from 135th Street saw our birds coming, they chased their birds up. We call the ripping birds the bombardiers. They must be at least a hundred feet higher than their birds, and they kept going straight uptown.

*****

Sarge was leading the way toward the George Washington Bridge; it was a field trip for the future leaders of the bombardiers. And behind the leaders were Ripley, Sandy, Vicki, Lucas, and a couple of flights that decided to tag along. They flew between Amsterdam and Broadway, passing half a dozen stocks along the way. Now they were making a left, heading toward the river, over the waters of the Hudson River, and the youngsters looked down at the liquid earth.

"That is not drinking water," said one of the elders.

The bombardiers followed the river's edge on the right concrete city, and they were now approaching the George Washington Bridge. It was huge up close, thought the young bombardiers, as it stretched across the Hudson. The traffic also flowed in opposite direction. All of a sudden, a high screeching sound came from behind them, and an invisible force of panic hit the birds all at once.

Sarge doubled his speed, and a gap appeared between him and his troop. The bombardiers quickly followed his lead. Sarge led them under the bridge, seeing seagulls flying off the bridge. Ripley quickly flipped over on his back and took a look above. Sandy asked, "What do you see?"

"Nothing," said Ripley and he flipped over again. Following Sarge, the bombardiers always flew over the bridge. Sarge had no idea how noisy it was under the bridge. There was a metallic clanking sound as the traffic flowed above. Down below sat a small red lighthouse at the edge of the water.

Sarge led the birds down to the water's edge, zooming around the lighthouse and flying upward on the other side of the bridge. They continued going up, and Ripley and Sandy were in the middle of the pack and heard the sweet sound of wing flapping. Flying away from the river, Sarge sensed the danger had passed. He flew across Upper Manhattan toward the East River, and a couple of stocks beneath them were also flying over their territory. Reaching the East River, they made a turn, and the bombardiers could see the water tower that sat right across from their home.

Sarge hollered, "If you can see it, it means you're never lost."

*****

Ray stood in front of the roof looking through the binoculars and catching up with the bombardiers coming from uptown. Hearing his name being called, Ray turned his head. It was Stanley, with his birds flying up above. Getting Ray's attention, Stanley was pointing upward toward Jersey. There he saw a big bird hovering over the stock on Riverside Drive. Ray was sure anyone who was flying birds at this moment was looking in that direction. He looked through the binoculars and saw that it was a bird of prey, all right. It didn't appear to be a hawk, and he knew what they look like. This bird, however, had long and narrow wings. *It must be a falcon*, he thought. *But this is hawks' territory, and this falcon is on the hunt.*

Forgetting about the birds that were coming back, Ray focused his attention on the falcon. He had heard stories about their attacks but never really actually witnessed one. All of a sudden, the falcon leapt forward and dove straight down. Ray felt his heart racing as he continued to watch. The birds from Riverside began to scatter in every direction—every bird was on his own. He thought he saw a puff of smoke in the sky, but it really was a bunch of feathers suspended in midair. It happened so fast, and now Ray could see the pigeon under the falcon being carried off.

Stanley hollered to Ray from across the roofs, "Did you see that?"

Looking through the binoculars again, Ray was stunned by what he just witnessed. As he watched the falcon across the river, he thought it was not a pretty sight.

*****

As the ripping birds were approaching, the rest of the stock was now hitting the roof. But Snowflake refused to land. Ray said, "Oh no," as he started to chase the birds up. She went up to meet the returning birds. She flew up to Ripley and said, "You went to the bridge without me."

Sandy, who was flying next to Ripley, asked her, "Did you see it? Did you see it?"

Snowflake replied, "Yes, it was a beautiful flight plan."

"No," said Ripley. "Did you see that bird get killed?"

"What bird?"

"The bird from Riverside. That falcon fell on that bird like a brick."

Now circling the roof, Sarge was leading the bombardiers down to the roof. Coming in from the left and hitting the landing pad, Ripley proceeded to tell the rest of the birds about what just happened.

"There's a new danger in the sky," Rufus was telling everyone. "You must keep your eyes open." Ray looked over the birds to make sure that they were all there and every bird was accounted for. Feeling a little queasy at what just happened, he couldn't wait for Danny or Corky to come up to the roof so he could tell them what he saw. Back on the water tower, the red flight and the crow witnessed the attack.

The red flight decided it was time to join the stock, but it was not going to be easy because his wing was throbbing and swollen. The crow, saw Red Hesitating and said matter-of-factly, "Look on the bright side. At least, you're going down and not trying to fly up." Trying to leave, the crow added, "One more thing, word is that they escaped from a zoo up north and they are heading toward warmer climates. They are just passing through. My name is Joe the Crow, by the way," the black bird said. "And you are?"

"I'm Red. Thanks for the information," and Red leapt off the water tower. He decided to circle down to the roof slowly; that way it wouldn't be too much strain on his wing.

Ray noticed that the red flight was having a little trouble trying to navigate his way in, and he opted to land on top of the screen, which had a larger space to land on. He noticed that he landed awkwardly but made it. Nova went over to greet him, and he proceeded to tell her the story. Nova listened while looking at the youngsters.

Red was now surrounded by Sarge, Rufus, and Clyde. Listening to the red flight, Rufus said, "We must be alert at all times, but we must continue to fly."

"That is our nature," said Sarge, and they all agreed. In unison, they chanted "Fly higher, fly longer, and fly farther forever!"

The red flight flew down to the roof floor and into the screen, which was open. Ray closed the screen door so he couldn't get out and went inside and grabbed him to have a look at his wing, but there was nothing broken.

Ray told Red, "You won't be flying for a while. You have to stay in the screen and let your wing heal." Ray came out of the screen and picked up his binoculars and began to scan the sky over Jersey. He noticed a lot of activities over the trees. *Those are not seagulls*, he thought. *They are birds of prey*. He counted four, turned around, and then sat down to watch the birds.

*****

Some time went by, and it was a beautiful day with blue skies. Ray noticed the birds from a hunt at Thirty-fifth Street were up and flying. He also noticed a single bird above their stock, which looked like a stray, and it was flying away from them. Jerry must've seen the stray, as his birds were now going up. Not to be outdone, Ray hurried

---

[2]   Picture from a book.

to the front of the roof and waved his hands up, and the birds took off. All three stocks were flying over their territory, fighting for this bird attention. The stray was now flying over Jerry's territory, and it looked like a blue tippet. It was coming down between our stocks. Sarge knew that Ray wanted this stray. Both brothers were on the roof looking up, trying to snare this stray. Sarge pushed his troop closer into Jerry's territory.

Both stocks just missed each other by a few feet. Circling, coming around again and going in the same direction, the stray was caught in the middle as our birds collided with Jerry's. They blended into one big tornado in the middle of the block. One building and a street that separated us and three buildings over was Jerry's roof. Someone was going to lose some birds today. The question is who?

While Corky and I were playing basketball, Corky saw what was happening, and he brought it to my attention. So we called a timeout and quit the game and started running toward our building. Ray was watching with excitement and anticipation and heard the skylight door open as Corky and I walked onto the roof and joined him. We looked up as both stocks tried to push each other into their territory. Sarge was waiting for the right angle to disengage with his wingmen flying beside him. As for the youngsters, this was their first clash. It could be scary being separated from the ones you know and with strangers trying to impose their will on you.

Everything they learned down in the basement was being put to the test. They kept their eyes on the leader as they jockeyed for position as they swayed and hooked. The neighborhood was alive with music. They didn't have much to say to each other than "Hello," "How've you been?" and "Welcome back." This was their first encounter for the youngsters flying with strangers. Ripley found Sandy, and up above was Snowflake, Nova, was beneath them pushing them up there to find more and more of their friends.

The bombardiers were starting to race to the top. As they did this, the rest of the troops started to dominate the top half of this huge tornado. Now the bottom half was mostly Jerry's birds, and the top half was now flying higher and, with each turn, getting closer to our territory. The separation was complete, and our birds were hooking and swaying back and forth over our roof: Ray turned toward us and started to tell us what he witnessed.

As we took our eyes off the birds, Corky asked, "Are you sure it was a falcon?"

"Yes, I'm sure." We all glanced at our birds as Ray continued. He picked up the binoculars and passed it to Corky and told him to look toward Jersey as he pointed in the direction he last saw the falcon.

Corky was looking through the binoculars with his big Afro. "They look like seagulls to me," said Corky.

"Seagulls don't hover over trees," said Ray.

"Whatever they are, there four of them." Corky passed the binoculars to me, and I looked through them. I don't know if I could really tell whether they were falcons or hawks, but I knew they were big.

Ray continued, "I thought I heard a small explosion when the falcon hit the bird. I saw a puff of smoke, which actually was its feathers." He had our attention.

"You should've seen it. It was beautiful and ugly at the same time. But no, you had to go down and play basketball," Corky interrupted him.

"I see the red flight came down from the water tower. It has a bum wing," said Ray.

"I'm going to keep it inside for a while. You're gonna need a month for those flight feathers to grow back," I told him.

"Well, a month it is. Let's not let him out, okay, fellas?"

"You got it."

We started to focus on the birds coming down. I was looking for Sandy and Ripley and Snowflake, and I saw them as they landed on the landing pad. Corky asked, "Did we lose any?" All of a sudden, we heard smacking of the wings coming from Jerry's direction and saw a Canadian and one of Corky's youngsters landing on our roof. We looked over our birds to make sure we didn't lose any. Then we noticed four new birds on the ledge.

Ray said, "He got this," so we backed up to let Ray do his thing. It did take a little skill and timing. The first thing he did was to grab a handful of food and start throwing it in the direction of the holding pen. The trapdoor at the bottom was held open by a string, and so was the top one. Ray was trying to direct them close enough to the trapdoor. As he held onto the string that held the trap door open, one of the birds was close to the trapdoor—a blue baldy with a white face and dark-colored body, like an American Eagle; and the other was a Teagle flight with a blend of red and white feathers, which was right behind the baldy. Ray fed them right into the trapdoor and pulled the string, and the trapdoor swung downward, pushing the two birds into the screen.

"You're the man, Ray," said Corky. There were two more to go, and one flew back to them. Corky and I could see they were watching. Ray snatched the other one when it went to drink.

"Who's the man!" he shouted as he put the yellow flight inside the screen and locked the door. "Who' the man!" While he was bragging a fast Spanish song came on the radio, who's the man!

"You are!" we shouted. Ray started celebrating, twisting and turning. His arms flailed all over the place.

Corky asked, "What are you doing?"

He said, "Doing my mambo dance." Corky and I started laughing. We laughed so hard we found ourselves on the floor. We told him to stop as we lay on the roof with tears in our eyes. Ray stopped dancing, turned around, and hollered at Jerry, "We got three!"

Jerry hollered, "They'll be back!"

"I'm going to keep them in for two weeks," Ray said. "They don't like losing birds to us, and we don't like losing birds to them. But that's part of the game."

"Time goes fast when you're having fun. That is so true," said Little Joe.

Well, it was getting dark again, and it was time to close up and put the birds to sleep. I noticed Ripley and Snowflake getting chummy with each other. All the birds were flying into the coop now, except Sandy. She was on top of the screen.

"What are you waiting for, Sandy?" I asked as I approached her, and she flew to the landing pad.

Ray asked me, "What's wrong with your bird?"

"I don't know."

"Maybe she wants to go home with you," said Corky.

"Come on, sweetie. Get inside, Sandy! Get inside the coop before the cat gets you." She flew into the screen and into the coop. I remember Ray saying, "She flew inside like she knew what you was saying."

"I don't know about you and that bird," said Corky.

"You're just jealous." It had been a while since all three of us locked up the birds together. We put the metal plate against the doorframe and then the locks and then we headed toward the skylight.

When we went down into the streets, we bumped into Jerry and Stanley, who were coming down the block. "You caught two of my birds," said Jerry.

Ray told him, "No, it was three."

"One of them was a stray," said Stanley.

"Which one?" Ray asked.

"The red Tiga," said Stanley.

"It was crazy the way the falcon caught that pigeon. That was the first time I witnessed a bird of prey making a kill," said Ray.

Jerry told us that he bumped into the guys from Riverside the other day, and they told him, "Those falcons were getting closer every day. They know there are plenty of birds here."

Ray asked, "What can we do about the falcon?"

Jerry said, "Let nature take its course."

I told them, "I caught a beautiful white tiplit the other day. We saw it flying with your birds. Early bird catches the worm."

"I can dig that," said Stanley. "By the way, how much do you want for that crazy tumbler?"

"He's not for sale," said Corky.

"I guess we just have to catch him," said Jerry.

"When we do, we will sell him back to you. Do you want to buy your birds back?" asked Corky.

"No," said Jerry. "We don't want those traders." We said our goodbyes and then went our separate ways.

Ray had to make up some time at the store for spending the day with us, and Corky went home to eat dinner and watch *Star Trek*.

*****

From her cubbyhole up above, Nova was looking down on Snowflake. "There is something strange about her."

"Who?" asked Clyde.

"Snowflake. She's just young and enthusiastic," said Clyde.

"She does have amazing' flying skills for such a young bird, but where did she come from? Did anybody bother to ask?"

"Well, if you must know," said Clyde, "I'll talk to Ripley. They seem to be getting friendly."

The bombardiers were gathered down below, discussing the dynamics of flying. Snowflake had the floor, telling the young bombardiers about her favorite "Arial" maneuvers and angle of descend. Snowflake noticed Nova looking down at her with curiosity.

CHAPTER 9

The Iron Bird

I woke up early. While I was having breakfast, I was watching the weatherman on TV saying we were going to have perfect weather for the next four days. I said good morning to everyone and headed out. Walking up the avenue, I could see Stanley's birds on the ledge of his roof. I should've kept my mouth shut about early bird catching the worm. I ran up the stairs and walked through the skylight door. It was a beautiful day with a few clouds. Looking over the coop, making sure no one had tried to get in, I proceeded to let my birds out. I took off the metal plate and laid it on the floor, and here they come—a flood of birds trying to be the first one out. I opened up the trapdoors.

I noticed that Ray left his binoculars behind the coop. I picked up the binoculars, and the first thing I did was to look toward Jersey. I didn't see anything that was not true. I saw Palisades Park and trees of green. At night, Palisades Park would come to life with its big Ferris wheel going around and around and with beautiful colored lights. It made me feel happy. It had a calming effect. It wasn't as big as the Ferris wheel at Coney Island but just as beautiful.

I went downstairs to get some fresh water. Cassondra answered the door with her long ponytail and red pajamas. She looked cute, and I was wondering why I hadn't asked her out. "Good morning," I said, and she told me she was going to start charging me for waking her up so early in the morning. She said it with a smile. As I walked past her, Peewee came and led me into the kitchen. I guess he knew my routine. That was one smart dog.

When I got to the roof, the oldest brother, Jerry, was on the roof waving at me, hollering, "Top of the morning to you. Do you have something for me?"

I hollered back, "Yeah, a falcon."

I fed the birds and looked for my favorite. "Where is Sandy?" I actually panicked for a few seconds when I didn't see her, and when I turned around, I saw that she was on top of the skylight looking down on the roof. "Hey, sweetie, what you doing up there?" I walked toward her. I raised my arm, and she flew onto my hand. I was a little amazed by that. I started rubbing the top of her head with my index finger, and after a few seconds, she flew down and joined the birds.

I let them chill out on the roof for a while, and I heard Jerry chasing his birds up.

*****

Sarge was talking to Rufus. "Where shall we go today? It's a beautiful flying weather. I feel like stretching out today. What about you, my old buddy?"

"Who are you calling old?" Rufus replied. "Some of the young bombardiers want to go to see the iron bird coop. Sandy has them all riled up. Let's ask Clyde." He was nearby and heard the conversation between his two old friends. They looked at him, and he nodded his head yes.

*****

Looking around, I noticed Sarge, Rufus, and Clyde were on top of the coop. I was wondering what they were cooking up, and then I saw Ripley fly to them.

*****

Ripley asked Sarge, "Can we go see the iron bird coop today?"

Sarge told him the flight plans for today. Ripley flew down to tell his sister and the bombardiers that they were going to see the iron bird coop. The bombardiers chanted, fly farther, higher, and harder. "Why can't anybody get that right?" said Sarge.

"Whichever way they say it, it still sounds good to me," said Rufus.

*****

The bombardiers were forty-four birds who loved to rip. Sometimes they would rip in bunches and go in different directions. Jerry's birds were coming down. I picked up the pole and chased the birds off, making that right-hand turn at the corner building and now flying over my head as they circled, going higher and higher. I noticed about fifteen birds were starting to rip away from the rest of the stock, and off they went. I wondered if the bombardiers didn't like flying in circles. When they ripped, they went straight like they knew where they were going.

It looked like they were heading toward Queens. I picked up the binoculars and started tracking them. They looked so beautiful flying together like homers. Farther and farther they were now so far away. They look like tiny gnats. I put the binoculars down and started looking up, watching the birds hooking and swaying. A black Tiga was tail-sitting. All of a sudden, Lucas started tumbling down. He must have tumbled at least seventy feet before breaking out of it. He was one amazing bird. I hoped he knew what he was doing. I looked over toward Jerry. He was watching Lucas, too, and he hollered at me, "That's one crazy bird."

I wondered where the bombardiers were going.

*****

As they were passing the East River and entering Queens, Sandy asked her father, "Are we there yet?"

Clyde was hypnotized with the sound of the flapping wings of his troops. "Will be there shortly," he said. "It's a lot farther than you thought."

"Yes, it is," said Sandy. Ripley, playing mother hen, asked Sandy if she was tired, and she replied, "No, silly, I'm not tired." She turned her head around to see if she could see her home, but she couldn't. Then she saw the water tower, which gave her some comfort.

As they forged ahead, the black flight with his white tips caught up with Sarge, asking him on our way back, "Could we swing towards the east side?" asked the black fight. My sister and I were separated at the pet shop. I caught a glimpse of her right before going down to the basement last summer. Sarge thought this could be a good lesson for the youngsters. "It sounds like a plan," said Sarge. The flight hollered, "Fly farther, fly harder, fly higher!" which gave inspiration to the birds that were following.

Sandy looked down and saw cars going in the opposite direction. The sun was warm, and there was a slight head wind. She felt the muscles in her shoulders getting stronger. And there it was, straight ahead, the iron bird lying there on the tarmac. And what is this? She saw people entering the iron bird. As they flew by and turned to the right, one of those iron birds were taking off. The noise terrified them. They turned to the left, and the sound just got louder. They flew faster, trying to get away from it. The iron bird lifted up, and the sound subsided.

As they were heading home, they could see the Hudson River and Jersey in the distance. It was small, but they could see the water tower and the projects looking down on the traffic on the expressway. They headed toward the bridge and passed Randolph Island. There was a stadium filled with hundreds of people listening to music. They were soon to be crossing East River. Sandy thought she wouldn't be asking to see the iron bird coop anytime soon; once was enough.

*****

The birds were now entering the east side of Manhattan. Back on the roof, the birds were now on the ledge. I started looking to see which ones were missing. I noticed most of the youngsters were gone. The bombardiers had been gone a long time. They were now in the east side of Manhattan. Sarge knew as soon as they were spotted. There would be three different stocks of birds each with more than one hundred birds coming at them. The young bombardier would keep their distance but close enough so that Black could spot his sister.

*****

Sarge and the black flight went down for a closer look. All three stocks were within a ten-block radius. Sarge could see all three coops, and the trainers were all pointing up to the bombardiers in the far-off distance. They know who we were. We were the birds from the upper West side that always came down this way to taunt them with our flying skills.

"There she is," said the black flight. She was in the middle stock as all three stocks below circled their territory. The black flight went down to get her attention. Sarge kept his distance flying circles high above the three stocks. Black sister managed to fly on the outer rim of her stock. Black was trying to keep his distance. The stock made a quick turn toward him.

As Sarge was watching what was happening to Black, he suddenly realized he wasn't alone. A group of birds were flying above and below him. They called themselves the dragons, and they were trying to convince Sarge to tell the bombardiers to come down a little closer so they could have a better look at them. As he tried to get away from them, they surrounded Sarge. From up above, they saw what was happening. Clyde and Rufus gave instructions to one of the Canadian tiplits to take the young bombardiers home.

Clyde and Rufus tilted their wings to the left and headed downward to try to rescue Sarge. The dragons were trying to bring Sarge down to their roof. They were a tough bunch being raised between two stocks, and they managed to be the best of the three, hardly ever losing a bird to the other two. Every time Sarge tried to make a move, a dragon would block his way. The three stocks below were starting to rise high and higher. There must be close to five hundred birds down below, each stock hooking and swaying. Clyde and Rufus knew what to do—a game of chicken was in order.

They went after the dragons with all the speed they could muster, attacking from the rear, and the dragons saw them, zooming straight down at them. They were not up for the game, and they politely got out the way. Clyde and Rufus flew right through the dragons. Sarge was with his two wingmen. They were heading down, trying to turn left and run into 150 birds hooking. The trainers below saw these three birds ripping right through their stock.

All three friends swung upward, and their wings speed increased as they flapped away and kept their eyes focused on the water tower. Clyde hollered, "Where's Black?"

"He'll come back," said Sarge as they flew to the West, seeing the young bombardiers in the distance.

They knew that they ruffled some feathers. This was the closest that Sarge ever came to getting caught. Rufus looked back and saw Black being consumed by the middle stock.

*****

On the roof, I noticed the birds from the east side, all three stocks, were up and flying. I picked up the binoculars to see what was going on. Oh no, I could see a small group of birds flying away from the east side. Knowing that the bombardiers may be in trouble, I chased the birds up, hoping the bombardiers would see their friends were waiting for them.

Looking through the binoculars, I couldn't make out who was who, but I knew they were coming home. I heard the skylight door open, and I turned around and saw that it was Ray. I told him that the bombardiers flew in the direction of Queens on the way back they must've drifted toward the east side, they'd been gone for a long time. They were coming from the east side, and Ray took the binoculars, and I started looking in that direction.

As the Canadian triplet was leading bombardiers home, Ripley asked the Canadian, "Shouldn't we go back for them?"

"Don't worry, Ripley. They are the leaders of this stock. They'll be back."

"I am leading this group home." Ripley veered to the right, and Sandy followed, as well as Snowflake. But before they could get too far, there was Clyde, Rufus, and Sarge flying hard toward them. The rest of the bombardiers turned around, and now Ripley and Sandy started rolling.[3] The bombardiers were zigzagging all over the place.

*****

---

[3] somersault while flying straight.

Ray and I were watching them through the binoculars, and Ray was complaining that they were moving too fast. The stock up above was hooking and swaying, and the tails sitters started parachuting down. Lucas was doing short tumbles, and the stock was swinging and rolling now.

We watched the bombardiers regroup under a beautiful blue skies right over our heads. Ignoring the stock, they started to come down as they circled the roof. They didn't waste any time; they wanted to feel the roof under their feet. They made a half circle at the back of the roof, and from that angle, they started cascading down to the front of the roof, which was pretty cool to look at. The bombardiers were a bunch of cool…birds.

The rest of the birds were flying overhead, and Ray and I started looking the bombardiers over to see if we lost any. They were all accounted for, and now the rest of the birds were starting to come down from the left and land on the roof edge.

Jerry hollered Ray's name. He didn't chase his birds up; this time, he was watching the action, so he hollered, "How many did you lose?"

Ray shouted back, "None," and he waved his arm down like we were lying. He just couldn't believe that our birds were that smart, but we knew differently. Ray said, "Hold it, the black flight is missing." The black flight belonged to Corky, and we started to scan the blue skies for him and look through the binoculars. No sign of him.

I hollered to Jerry, "We are missing one." Jerry was now chasing his birds up, which was a good thing. If the black flight was out there, he should definitely notice Jerry's stock.

Ray said, "If the black flight appears, he's going to chase up! We shouldn't have to."

I said, "If he comes back from the east side, do you think he's gonna land on their roof?"

Ray said, "You're right about that," so he sat down on the roof floor with his back against the wall. His hand was full of big kernels of corn, which he got from the pigeon food. He was flicking the kernels with his fingers, trying to get it over the wall of the building for home run. I joined him, and we made a game out of it, playing and talking. Ray said that Stanley chased twice as much as we did. Then he added, "I like the birds to feel like the roof is their home and not always being chased off it." I agreed.

He beat me, 10 to 9. Time went by, and Ray was walking the roof, looking down in the alley. I was at the front looking down on the avenue. Sometimes you forget there are people outside, buses and cars going up and down the hill. There was also a softball game in the schoolyard. Being on the roof felt like it was our world, that the skies belonged to us. It was a beautiful day with just the right amount of clouds for some shade. I heard Ray call me and I looked in his direction.

"Look at this," he said, and I walked over to him. He was pointing down to the alley. I looked over the wall, and Ray was pointing to a window. There a young red and white Tiga was on the window sill listening to Jamaican music.

We often heard all types of music coming from the alley, and we stood there looking. All of a sudden, the skylight door opened it was Cassondra with sandwiches in her hand and two cans of soda walking toward us. She handed me a sandwich and soda, I told her thank you, and she asked, "What are you looking at?"

"A bird on the windows," she said.

"Yeah, right," she looked over to the wall and said, "Your got a Rastafarian bird," as she gave Ray his sandwich and soda, and then she said the other day she was watching the karate movie and one of our birds was on her window watching the movie with her.

Ray said, "Really!"

She started laughing as she walked to the front of the roof to look at the birds.

"Up and away, up and away," said the girl in the ponytail.

This is my building with the water tower on top.

Ray decided to chase the young red tiga off the windowsill below, and it flew through the alley and came around and landed on the roof with the rest of the birds. Cassondra stood on the roof for a while, telling us to chase up. She wanted to see that crazy bird named Lucas. I gave her the bamboo pole and told her to run it against the edge of the roof and to say, "Up and away, up and away." Ray was trying not to laugh. I walked the birds up to the ledge, and Sandy flew over my head and landed on the skylight.

I told Cassondra to do it now while holding the pole with both hands, and she started moving across the roof, saying, "Up and away! Up and away!" I started laughing, and she asked us, "Why are y'all laughing?"

I told her, "We've never seen a girl chasing up the birds before." Jerry saw our birds going up, and he chased his birds off the roof. We no longer worried about our birds colliding with his. Both stocks kept their distance while they hooked and swayed to the music, circling their territory.

Cassondra looked up at the birds, waiting for Lucas to do his thing. He did not fail her and he started tumbling head over tail straight down. It must've been about twenty feet before he broke out of it, and he flew back up to the stock. She asked, "Why does he do that?" Ray told her it's in his blood, and she said, "It's a good thing he knows when to stop." She told me that she had to go down to help her mother start dinner and that they were having relatives come over. "See you later," she said and left.

As we were watching our birds, we heard the skylight door on the other roof opening slowly. Ray and I were watching to see who was coming through the door, and it was Corky trying to sneak up on us. I told him, "You're busted," as Corky got closer.

Ray told him, "You missed it," as he was turning around, heading toward the skylight door.

Corky asked Ray, "Where're you going, and what did I miss?"

Ray tried to sound sophisticated. "To answer your first question, my man, I'm going to work. To your second question, Danny lost your bird."

"Thanks a lot, Ray."

As he entered the skylight, I could hear Ray laughing as he walked down the stairs. Corky looked up at me from the other roof, asking which one, and I told him it was the black flight. The bombardiers went ripping straight toward Queens, coming back. They must have drifted toward the east side. He didn't come back with them. "That's messed up," he said. "He's one of my favorite birds, so the guys from the east side got him."

"Yup!" Corky climbed up to our roof and looked up at the birds. Lucas gave Corky something to smile about. From way up above, he started tumbling, one of the longest tumbles so far. I could see Corky was a little sad, wondering what happened to his black flight.

I told him, "You're black flight will be back." Corky spent $10 on that bird last summer, and it was one of the most expensive birds he ever bought. Corky asked, "You sure Jerry didn't catch him?" I said no and told him their stock was down when the bombardiers came back.

We talked for a while doing repairs on the screen and cleaning up the roof. We always kept a clean roof, and we heard Jerry hollering, "Falcon! Falcon!" He was pointing toward the river, and we saw it—the birds from Riverside were down. The falcon was hovering over riverside, and it had companion—there were two. The birds from 135th were up and flying, Jerry's birds were down, and so were ours.

Corky and I climbed up on top of the skylight so we could get a better view, and we could almost see their coop. Corky jumped off the skylight to get the binoculars from the top of the pigeon coop, and he tossed me the binoculars. I gave him a hand up, and we could see them gliding, coming closer as they were now crossing Broadway high above choo-choo birds. I saw Dannyboy was up there with him, and he was trying to encourage his birds to come down. His birds hadn't noticed the falcons gliding. Suddenly the Falcon dove straight down it was fast. The Falcom has his eyes on one bird, just as Ray described it, as I continue looking through the binoculars.

I could see the falcon's wings tucked in, looking like a saber jet. I could almost make out his features on his face—those big eyes and the beak a hundred times bigger then a pigeon's, and at the end of his beak was a hook. I saw him extend his legs out with those big claws right then and there. Feathers were floating down from the impact. He must have not had a good grip, as the birds slipped away. It was sad to see one of his wings being mangled as he tried desperately to fly away, and right before my eyes, the other falcon scooped him up. I couldn't believe what I was seeing; it was nature at its cruelest. Choo-choo birds were flying all over the place, hightailing it out of their territory.

I took a quick look at our birds, hoping they wouldn't suddenly take off. I didn't think they knew what was going on. The falcons were now crossing the river, and I gave the binoculars to Corky, who said, "I can see the birds under the wings of the falcon. He has his big talents wrapped around the bird."

I looked over to Jerry, and he was just shaking his head back and forth. Half of the choo-choo birds were flying over our territory, and I saw Jerry running toward the front of his roof, chasing his birds up and trying to catch some choo-choo birds. Corky jumped off the skylight and did the same. I felt bad for choo-choo and his birds, but all is fair in love and war and to the victor goes the spoils, and the falcon won again.

While Corky was trying to catch choo-choo birds, I was in deep thought, wondering when it was going to be us (and all the people down in the street that missed what was happening above the roof).

Corky was happy now that he caught three birds—one tiplet and two flights. Corky hollered to Jerry, "I got three," and Jerry hollered back, "I have four." Corky turned around and looked at me and said, "You know it could happen to us." I said, "I know. It wasn't that dark, and the birds were on top of the screen, wanting to go inside the pigeon coop. Corky put his three brand-new birds inside the pigeon coop and opened up the trapdoors so they could get inside. This was definitely the easiest lockup we ever did.

*****

There was a lot of chatter among the birds. Sarge approached, one of the three strangers that were there, a yellow flight, told Sarge that they came out of nowhere. His companion, a blue baldy, said, "They must've been hiding in the clouds."

"I can't stopped shaking," said the Brown flight.

Sarge said, "You can stay with us if you want, or you can leave when they let you out.

"When would that be?" one of them asked.

"In a couple of days."

"That sounds good to me," said the yellow flight.

The brown flight said, "Let's make it a week."

Up above in their crate, Clyde was telling Nova it was a good thing that we didn't fly in that direction.

Ripley said, "That doesn't make a difference. We are usually the first coop to open up, and we out there by ourselves."

Clyde thought out loud, saying to himself, "The early bird catches the worm."

Nova asked Clyde, "What did you say?"

Sandy interrupted by saying, "D will not let that happen to us."

"What can he do?" said Ripley as he was flying down to Snowflake and the rest of the bombardiers.

"Does anyone have any ideas?" Ripley asked as he addressed the group. Everyone shook their heads.

"I have one," said Rufus from above. "But I'm still working on it."

Lucas said, "I have an idea. Fly higher, fly farther, and fly harder."

Sarge said, "That's exactly what we're gonna do."

Everyone in the coop cheered.

*****

Corky and I went to the corner store where Ray worked and told him what we saw.

Day 5, the next morning, Corky and I met on the roof. Corky asked me how I slept, and I said I slept okay. I asked him, and he replied, "I went to sleep with that falcon on my mind," as he went to open up the coop.

I went down to fetch some fresh water, and when I came up, I told Corky that Cassondra heard that a lot of people witnessed two big birds killing a pigeon and that the people were talking about it in the street.

I told Corky the only one who was really safe was the Dutchman. Corky replied, "Why? Is it because he was farther away?"

"No, because he has the laziest birds in the world, but he's still catching and selling."

Corky said, "Do you remember those days when we used to buy birds from the Dutchman and they always went back to him?" Yup' I remember, having a bunch of fancy fantail chilling on the roof is pretty slick. He was not on the roof that often anymore, and he still caught strays and went up a couple of times a day to make sure they had enough food and water and to see if any stray bird landed on his roof."

I told Corky I didn't want to lose any birds to those falcons, and he said, "Me either."

"The birds look pretty chirpy this morning."

Corky said, "That's because they went to bed early." Corky got the pole and chased them up, and off they went. They were flying nice and tight, and the first chase up was the best. As music was playing on the radio, they started hooking from right to left in a deep swinging motion. It was a beautiful morning, and not too far away, we could see a stock of homers going across the horizon, heading uptown. They sure were in a hurry, and our birds were high above us. Now the bombardiers were starting to rip away from the stock, but it was mostly the youngling—Ripley, Sandy, Snowflake, Charlie the Rastafarian, Lucas, and a few others—and a couple of Canadian triplets. Clyde was telling Nova that they were better off ripping far from here. They'd be much safer.

CHAPTER 10

The Dutchman

In this picture, you can see Corky's black flight. Up above flying is Sandy, and the four birds on the edge are Vicki, Red, Snowflake, and Bingo. Down below is that tumbler named Lucas. The picture below is of the red owl, and he is one good-looking bird. You can also see his boot feathers. To his left is a young homer, and to the right is yellow tiga flight.

Sarge knew by letting them go on their own, it would build confidence, and most of the adults knew it too. Sarge led his troops down from the back of the roof. They cascaded down to the front of the roof, and Corky said, "Look at that, it looks so cool." I told him that they did that the other day.

*****

The birds could sense the pride that the trainers had for them. A chorus of "Fly higher! Fly harder! Fly farther!" resonated through the stock. They could see that the boys were happy. Sarge shouted, "That's what good birds do when you treat them right. Well done."

*****

My eyes finally caught up with the younger birds as they ripped way, flying over the city college and now St. Nicholas Park. I noticed that the bombardiers were flying high over the Dutchman's territory and now flying circles over the Dutchman's roof.

*****

As the youngsters circled over the Dutchman's territory, Vicki said, "We are free to go in any direction. Where shall we go?"

Charlie, who was now a full-fledged Rastafarian who had his feathers tied up in dreads, said, "Let's go to Jamaica mohn. I hear it's beautiful this time of year."

He was interrupted by Penny, who hardly said anything at all. "You mean Jamaica Queens, don't you? the' girl can talk mohn," said Charlie. "My mother told me to mine my own business, keep up the good work mohn."

"This is Dutchman's territory," said Bingo, wanting everyone to be aware of it. Looking down on the roof, Sandy tell Snowflake, look at that beautiful pigeon house, let's go down and have a better look, come with me snowflake, I want to see it up close.

"Not without me," said Ripley.

"And me," said Lucas, who was also flying with them. As the rest of the young bombardiers headed toward Queens, Ripley said, we'll catch up.

As the four friends ventured downward, Lucas noticed these beautiful female birds. The boys couldn't take their eyes off them. Ripley and Lucas started waving their wings at them. The young bombardiers started gliding down slowly around the roof, and Lucas started tumbling. Snowflake said to Sandy, "What a show-off." Instead of Lucas coming up to meet them, they went down to meet Lucas, which brought them much closer to the roof.

The Dutchman birds seemed happy to see them.

Lucas said, "There is no Dutchman on the roof. Let's drop down for a visit."

"I don't know," said Ripley.

Sandy said, "We could land on the beautiful pigeon coop if someone comes up."

"We just fly away." Ripley wanted to go down. "Just stay away from trapdoors," said Ripley.

Snowflake added, "And don't drink the water."

Sandy led the way, and they landed on top of the pigeon coop. This was the first time they had been on another roof, except for Lucas. They had taken a good look at the roof layout and noticed the door. If it opens, is time to go. They all agreed.

"Why don't you stay here with me, Ripley?"

This is what a fantail looks like.
They come in different colors.

---

4 Picture of a fantail from the Internet.

So they relaxed a little bit. A handsome owl with red wings and white body and a cap on his head flew up from the floor to the top of the coop to greet them, saying, "It's been a while since we had visitors. Welcome."

"This place is beautiful." Across the street, the park seemed to rise up to city college. Looking across a tsunami of green trees, Sandy said, "Can we take a closer look?"

"By all means," said the owl.

Sandy and Snowflake jumped off and landed on the platform that ran the length of the coop. It had windows large enough for a bird to fly in and out. They poked their heads inside. Ripley asked, "Who is that remarkable-looking bird on the ledge?"

The owl took a look and replied, "That's Venus. You look like someone I used to know. Who are your parents?"

"Clyde and Nova, that's my sister who's looking over your coop. I have to admit it is little different from what we are used to seeing. I can see the resemblance," said the red owl.

"Do you know my parents?"

"Yes," said the red owl. "We were all friends and your mother."

"Good," said Ripley. "We heard you used to be one of our leaders. Why do you remain here?"

"It's a long story. Ripley, don't talk to her."

"Who?"

"The fantail. You and your sister must leave this place." The owl slowly turned a round looking up in the direction of our home, said, "The fantail is a siren." The red owl turned his back on Ripley. Ripley couldn't take his eyes off her, and he flew to the ledge to talk to this remarkable-looking bird. "Hello," he said, landing as gracefully as possible.

"I'm Ripley and I believe I know your name."

"What's my name?"

Ripley replied, "It's Venus." He couldn't seem to take his eyes off her. Her gestures were so elegant and her voice so pleasant, the most beautiful voice he ever heard.

"I see your stock flying all the time. You guys are good." Her voice was music to his ears. It was heavenly and sounded like she was singing. "Why don't you stay here with me, Ripley?"

Ripley noticed Snowflake was staring at him from the platform on the coop, looking dreamy. He looked at Lucas, who was on the roof floor surrounded by pretty fantails of all colors, asking him to go back up and tumble for them.

*****

"Seeing those young birds land on the Dutchman's roof, I was very disappointed," I jokingly told Corky.

"Those were your dumb birds."

"You mean *our* birds, don't you?" He took a quick look up above and scanned the sky. "No falcon, and across Jersey, I saw nothing," and I proceeded to chase the birds up, knowing that they could see our stock from the Dutchman's roof there down below on the other side of the park.

*****

Venus's voice was in his ear. Looking at Snowflake, he thought, *Where is my sister?* Venus was telling Ripley to stay on the Dutchman's roof here with her. Snowflake didn't like what she was seeing or hearing, so she flew off the platform and landed between Ripley and Venus. She told Ripley that his sister was inside the Dutchman coop. That woke him up. He could still hear D's voice telling him to take care of his sister and him saying the words, "Aye, Captain!" out loud. Ripley quickly took off toward the pigeon coop, and Snowflake told Venus, "Excuse us." It time to go.

Ripley landed on the platform and poked his head inside the window. It was spacious and well constructive. He saw the roles of cubbyholes on top of each other and he called out her name. "Come down here," said Sandy, almost sounding like an echo. Ripley said no. All of a sudden, the roof door opened, and the Dutchman was on the roof. Lucas was startled and he flew straight up. Sandy felt the vibration and she panicked and flew out the pigeon coop and straight into the holding pen. She was terrified and she turned her head and saw the Dutchman walking by, looking like a locomotive engineer, and with the hat to boot. *So that's the Dutchman*, she thought as she was trying to push the trap door open from the inside. Ripley saw a head with a cap—the Dutchman. He ducked his head inside the coop and then he jumped in and flew in the direction of the holding pen. The Dutchman noticed the commotion inside the holding pen, and Sandy desperately tried to find a way out. Snowflake got the Dutchman's attention. She was going to try to buy some time for Sandy and Ripley.

Sandy remembered the spider's words. *Don't panic. I got it, I'll just go the way I came.* And when she went to turn around, Ripley was just putting on the brakes. Feathers were floating everywhere. Ripley told Sandy to calm down. "I am calm," she said.

"You weren't a few seconds ago."

"I'm beginning to like it here, but it's a little too dusty for me. Let me guess which way we're going," said Sandy.

"If you knew the way out, why are you still here?"

"I just wanted to see how much you loved me."

"Stop joking around. Let's go!"

Now Dutchman saw two birds inside the holding pen. Now his attention was on Snowflake, and the Dutchman moved like a cat. *I'm not selling this one*, he thought. Lucas was high above as he circled the Dutchman's roof. He saw his two friends inside the pen and wondered, *Why is Snowflake still on the roof?* He decided to tumble to take the attention away from Snowflake. The Dutchman looked up and watched Lucas do his thing. Then slowly the Dutchman picked up the water can, trying to get as close as possible to this white tiplit. Snowflake watched his every move. He put the water can down and walked away from it. Slowly, he started throwing some food in the direction of the water can. *You got to be kidding me*, thought Snowflake. She took her eyes off the Dutchman and looked at the platform where the windows were. She was hoping to see Sandy and Ripley come out flying.

Sandy and Ripley were backtracking and they flew back through the opening of the pigeon coop, heading upward toward the windows. Sandy flew out of one and Ripley out of another. The Dutchman turned his head, seeing the two birds escaping. Snowflake decided it was time to say goodbye to the Dutchman. As she flew backward off his roof, going straight up, his mouth dropped. All four bombardiers reunited high above the Dutchman's roof. Lucas gave him one last tumble, and they were on their way home. The Dutchman was not pleased, and he chased his birds up in anger. Ripley took one last look at Venus as he was flying home.

*****

On the roof, Corky was looking in the direction of the Dutchman's territory with the binoculars. And then I heard those sweet words, "They're coming back!" I knew once they saw the stock flying they'd come back. I asked for the binoculars looking through them, and saw who those birds were. Three of them were mine, and I had a smile on my face. I was feeling good again. As Lucas got closer from above, he did three short tumbles as he joined the rest of the flying birds overhead. And here comes the rest of the bombardiers, now coming into view. I took a quick look toward Jersey, but I didn't see anything. I waited for the birds to come down.

*****

When they landed, Snowflake started talking to Sandy. "You going inside the Dutchman's coop was not part of the plan. What were you thinking, Sandy?"

"I know. I should never have gone inside."

"You know you would've broken D's heart if you got caught. Thanks to Ripley," said Snowflake.

"I was about to leave the same way I went in before Ripley came."

"Okay, that's good, and you also put him in danger."

"I'm sorry, you're right. I'll never set foot on another roof ever again."

Farther down the landing pad, Ripley and Lucas were telling the rest of the bombardiers about the Dutchman as more birds gathered around to listen. Sarge came with a stick under his wings, as he walked toward the birds, they parted to let him through. He was hot when he reached Ripley and Lucas, who stood there looking at him seconds pass and Sarge asked, what were you're thinking?"

Lucas told him, "We were doing reconnaissance."

"Reconnaissance my feather," said Sarge. The young bombardiers were grounded for now.

Ripley said, "We know why the Dutchman is so notorious. He has these beautiful birds called fantail, and they do magic. They're siren, siren, siren."

"One siren is enough, Ripley. We do not fly over the Dutchman's territory. Is that clear? Do you understand?"

"Yes, sir." Sarge turned around and flew straight up, letting go of the stick. He caught it with his right claw. It wasn't over for Ripley and Sandy. Clyde and Rufus came, Sandy stepped in front of Ripley and told her dad it was her fault.

"I hope you learned your lesson, Sandy."

"I did," she replied.

Rufus asked, "Did you see a red owl."

"Yes, we did," said Ripley.

"Did you ask him why?"

"Yes, I did. He said it was a long story. It looks like he's under the siren spell."

"Does he look well?"

"Yes, he's a handsome fella."

"That's him, all right," said Rufus. "He was our friend."

Snowflake interrupted, "Here comes D. I have some choice words for them, which I am not going to repeat."

Corky said, "He's going home to have some lunch, and he will be stopping by Ray at the store to tell him what the bombardiers did to the Dutchman."

Sandy and Ripley at the center, and to the left of
Sandy is Snowflake. At the extreme right is Sarge.
"What were you thinking?" said Sarge.

CHAPTER 11

The Condor

So now it was just me and the birds. I was sitting by the wall, looking over. It was a six-foot drop to the next roof. It was the same thing for the two roofs to my right. It was a beautiful day, so I took a panoramic view of what was out there in front of me. All of a sudden, on this same wall that I'm sitting on, a horsefly jumped into my line of sight, vibrating with a buzzing sound that seemed to be amplified no more than two inches from my eyes, which made it look humongous. I quickly reacted, leaning my head back a little too far. I brought my hands to swat it away and lost my balance. I tilted over as I was beginning to fall backward. My legs were starting to rise, and I quickly slammed my hands back down. As I was grasping for the wall, my left hand slipped off. My right hand was glued to the edge of the wall as I went over and landed on my feet. *Damn horsefly, it could've killed me*, I thought, taking my hand off the wall. I started to chuckle, remembering how big it looked and the loud buzzing it made.

"It really must have been big for you to embarrass yourself like that," said Patty.

"It was as big as a half-a-dollar coin. Actually it was two big horseflies on top of each other. I also remember looking at my building and thinking how many people saw me slip off the roof and if anyone would tell my mother. It was too beautiful of a day to be indoors, so I started to climb back. Looking up to my left, I saw

Sandy and Snowflake looking down. 'Did y'all see that? I climbed up, regained my composure, and sat down. I'm glad the fellas weren't there. If they were, they would never let me forget it.' I could picture them laughing."

The sun was beaming, and I saw some shade by the skylight wall. I walked over and sat down against the wall with my legs stretched out. The sun was hitting the tip of my sneakers as I was watching the birds dip themselves in a big pan of water and step out to sunbathe. Sandy flew off the holding pen and flew in my direction, and I thought she was going to land on top of the skylight. She landed on my thigh. She came to join me in the shade, smart girl, and nestled on my legs, and I started gently rubbing her under her beak. My right arm was starting to hurt.

I closed my eyes just to rest them for a little bit and I must have dozed off. When I woke up, all the birds were in the shade, and most of them were lying down. I looked down, and Sandy was still on top of my legs, looking at me. I reached out to touch her, and she jumped on my hand. As I slowly got up to stretch, it seemed like all the birds were looking. Just to mess with them, I brought my hand with Sandy on it close to my lips. She let me kiss her on her beak. I gently nudged my hand outward, and she flew off and landed on the landing pad.

*****

Sandy couldn't seem to contain herself. She seemed to be walking in circles on the landing pad. Snowflake quickly landed beside her and said, "Calm down, girl. Everyone is watching."

"I don't care. He kissed me. D kissed me."

"I think everybody saw that, but they don't believe it was a real kiss," said Snowflake.

"It was a real kiss, and when he kissed me in those few seconds, I wasn't a pigeon."

"What were you?" asked Snowflake.

"I don't know. Do you even know what a kiss means?"

"Yes, I hear a lot about kissing all the time in the music that comes out the radio. When two people kiss, it means they are in love. Why does life have to be so cruel? It's playing a joke on me," Sandy said with tears in her eyes as she looked toward the open sky. Snowflake could hear her wishes.

*****

"It's past two o'clock," said the men on the radio, and I was getting hungry watching the birds lounging around and sunbathing. I decided to go down to the store and buy myself a large hero sandwich and stop by Cassondra's house. I closed the coop up and headed down to the store.

*****

Sarge was on top of the coop and he saw a crow on the water tower; it was Joe the crow. Thinking about what Lucas said about reconnaissance, Sarge told Rufus that he was going up to talk to the crow, and from what he heard from Red, the crow was approachable and pretty cool. So he took off straight up to the water tower. He went with no fear. He landed close to the crow and started walking toward him.

"Hello, are you Joe the crow?" asked Sarge.

"Yes, and who are you?" asked the crow.

"I'm Sarge. I am the leader of the stock of birds down below."

"How is Red?" asked the crow.

"He's mending nicely," answered Sarge. "Can I ask you to tell me about the falcons over Jersey?" Joe proceeded to tell him that the leader of the falcons was called Ramses. Since their escape, they had left a trail of destruction. They had done away with many birds. The sparrows had learned not to fly higher than the tallest tree, and the pigeons were forced to migrate somewhere else.

From here and all the way up to the bridge was their territory. They made a deal with the hawks. The four falcons called themselves the family, and their family had gotten bigger by two. The food supply was now on this side of the river.

Sarge asked, "Is there anything that they're scared of?"

Joe thought for a second. "The only thing I can think of is a condor, and they have not been seen around these parts in over one thousand years."

"This condor that you speak of, what does it look like?"

Joe spoke. "From what my father told me and his father told him, they had the biggest wingspan of all the birds, the largest thing in the sky since the dinosaur bird."

Sarge heard the crow's stomach grumbling. He asked, "Is there any baby bird down below?"

"No."

"Why don't you try some fish?" He hoped that his comments didn't anger the black crow.

"Those seagulls are greedy. They don't like sharing," said Joe. He continued, "Ramses and Karzai will be back."

"Karzai she is fierce. She has two chicks to feed." While Sarge was listening to Joe the crow, he was looking down on the roof. He noticed D was walking onto the roof. "Joe, I have to leave. It's been nice talking to you. By the way, do you like pigeon food?"

"Not if I can help it," said Joe the crow.

"There is always some leftover on the roof," said Sarge and he flew off the water tower and headed down to the roof.

*****

Ray came up for a couple of hours, and I went downstairs to play basketball. I told him to whistle when he was ready to leave, which he did. Corky came up later that evening to help me close up. He also brought a whistle with him. Maybe all the flyers in the hood should get one. Whoever sees the falcon first should start blowing the whistle. "That's a good idea," I told him.

"Whose idea was it?"

"Ray's."

"Yup." He crossed two roofs over, got Stanley and Jerry's attention and told him about the whistle. Jerry said in a loud voice, "It's a good idea."

We had no problems locking up the birds, no signs of the falcon, so it was a good day.

*****

Inside the coop, Clyde, who was talking to a friend, looked up toward Sarge's cubbyhole. All that could be seen were his tail feathers. In another part of the coop, Sandy and Snowflake were walking alongside Rufus. "Do you have something to say, ladies?" he asked.

"Yes, we both do." Sandy looked at Snowflake. "You first."

Snowflake asked Rufus, "How long are the bombardiers grounded for?"

"Maybe a few days or maybe a week. That should make you think twice before disobeying orders." He stopped. "What is your question, Sandy?"

"Why should the others pay for my mistake?"

"That's very noble of you. Your actions could've demoralized the stock and the trainers. The bombardiers are not about one or two birds or four, for that matter. The bombardiers represent who we are as a stock. I feel the pride the trainers have when the bombardiers are coming home, and when we hit the landing pad, I feel love radiating from them. I also feel their sadness when one of us is lost. We fly as a squadron, one unit, to answer your question, Sandy."

"Why are the others being punished? They failed to produce a leader. He walked away. I have never seen him so grouchy," said Sandy.

Later Snowflake found Ripley. "You said it was going to be fun. No one expected this to happen, you're not thinking of leaving, are you?"

"No," said Snowflake, a bombardier for life.

Music started to fill the coop. It was Charlie the Rastafarian bird playing his guitar, singing,

> So much trouble in the world,
> bless my eyes this morning.
> I get another chance to fly again
> the way that earthly things are going.
> Anything could happen,
> falcon sailing on their ego trips,
> trying to Stomp us every chance they could,
> one million miles from reality.
> No one cares for you
> and no one cares for me

"So much trouble in the world," all the birds sang chorus.

After a while, the singing died down. Clyde was wondering what Sarge was up to. He thought it must be important for him to turn his back on them. It was getting late, and everyone was in their cubbyhole. Everyone was saying good night to one another. Sandy whispered to Ripley, "Do you think those falcons will ever go away?"

"No," he said. "As long as there are pigeons on this side of the river, they're not going anywhere."

And off to sleep they went. Ticktock, ticktock. Morning came and we were waiting for someone to let us out. Sarge walked around like the inspector general. He sensed an attitude among the birds; regardless of what was out there, they were going to fly hard, fly high, and fly farther, and they were going to do it without fear. Being cooped up longer than usual will make you feel that way. Finally, there were vibrations on the roof floor. Someone was walking inside the holding pen. There was the sound of the locks being opened and a large beam sunlight and a rush of fresh air, which flared up every bird's nostril with a burst of energy. We were ready to go, but we only got as far as the holding pen. D made us wait for the trapdoors to be opened. Bingo had his eyes to the sky.[5]

---

[5] So much trouble in the world by Bob Molly, I changed a few words.

CHAPTER 12

Tumbling Lucas

Day 6

As I finished scanning the sky, I walked over to the screen to let them out. I could see they were anxious to fly. After I opened up all the trapdoors, they took off straight into the air without touching the roof. Rufus was telling the new birds, "It looks like today will be your day to make your decision." As they circled above and came into formation, they kept getting higher and higher with every turn. They leveled off and started swinging and hooking with the soulful rhythm that only belonged to them. I looked uptown and I noticed Stanley was on his roof getting ready to let his birds out. He stopped and started looking at our birds with admiration. One big ball of birds rolling around in the sky, nice and tight. I heard him whistling, so I turned, and he waved at me and I waved back. I looked at the coop. The trapdoors opened, and the plate was off the coop. I realized I let out choo-choo birds and Stanley's two birds. I hoped he didn't notice them.

I heard the skylight door opening; it was Ray and Corky. As they came closer, I told them that I let all the birds out by mistake. Corky asked me, "Are they flying with the stock?"

"Yeah," Ray said. Another exciting day in the neighborhood.

Corky said, "You think they'll go back?"

"We'll see when the birds come down." Ray and Corky waved at Jerry and Stanley, acting normal and cool, not wanting them to know that there were five new birds flying with our birds. Jerry took a quick look toward Jersey and then chased his birds up. Our birds were coming down with the five strays.

As Jerry's birds were going up, our birds circled gradually, coming lower, and some of the birds were smacking their wings, which sounded like clapping. The youngsters were starting to get playful. You could tell they were enjoying themselves. Then we noticed Lucas tumbling down and we waited for him to break out of it. He just kept coming down, and for a second, I thought he might hit the landing pad. He missed it by at least ten feet, and he disappeared below the roof. We all looked at one another.

Some birds were already on the landing pad and they were watching in horror as Lucas continued tumbling down. His father hollered, "Break out of it, son!" His mother turned her back; she didn't want to watch. All the birds were screaming at Lucas to stop! He was rotating so fast he couldn't break out of it. They watched Lucas disappear. We waited for Lucas to come back up to the roof, and when he didn't, we ran to the edge of the roof and started looking down. There was no sign of Lucas.

Ray looked at me and said, "That bird done killed himself." Lucas was not on the sidewalk, and he was not in the street. Corky got up and ran toward the skylight door, and I followed. We found ourselves in front of the building, expecting to find a dead bird. It seemed like nobody saw anything and everything seemed normal. Looking down the steps that led to the backyard—no signs of feathers. We looked between the cars and under them. I started looking at every fire escape in front of the building. I looked at all the fire escape on the block. I didn't see him. Where could he be?

"Don't tell us Lucas died, Mr. D," said little Joe.

"I know what happened to Lucas," said David. "The old lady finally got a pigeon soup."

"That's not funny," said Patty.

"No, that didn't happen," I said.

"The cats got him, right?" said Patty.

"No." When that happened to Lucas, I knew something strange was going on. I couldn't put my finger on it. I didn't want to mention it to the fellas because they'd think I was going crazy. But I felt something. Hesitating to speak, I got stuck looking at a fluffy cloud.

"Continue, Mr. D," said little David.

I was kneeling between two parked cars. I was just getting up from my knees as a car went by. Corky stood between two cars, and I looked at him nudging his shoulders. As he passed the back window of a red convertible, but something caught my eye. I focused on the back plastic window in the corner of the window. There was a rip, and it was dingy-looking. I saw a small shadow of a bird walking back and forth. I walked over to the back window and saw a tear. I called for Corky, who was working his way down the block. "You ain't going to believe this." I was pointing to the back window of the convertible, and his eyes grew large. "He's alive. Get out of town. He's alive"."

"No way," he said. "Unbelievable. How lucky can a bird get?"

Lucas struck a convertible, which happened to be in the right spot with windows made of plastic. It broke his fall, and in went Lucas. He must've hit it pretty hard because he busted through it. Even God loves Lucas. He was one of a kind. It was a miracle, I thought.

"Is he alive?" Ray shouted from above. Looking up, I saw Ray's face hanging off the ledge. I told him Lucas was inside a car.

"What! I'm coming down."

Corky asked, "How are we going to get him out of there?"

*****

On the roof, their sadness was turning into a celebration. Looking down, the birds cheered, "Who the man!" They shouted, "Lucas is the man!"

Clyde told Nova, just like in the basement.

*****

Ray must've run down. He walked to the back of the window and took a look. "I don't believe it, really." He looked straight up to the sky and down to the window. "Amazing."

"He looks okay," I said.

"Now how are we going to get him out of there? If we scare him, he will fly to the front of the car and drive off."

*****

Lucas was actually happy to see them but wondered how he got inside here. *How in the heck did I get here? Hurry up and get me out!*

*****

I told Ray to go to the front and put his hands on the windshield and Corky to the side window to the right. The hole was at the left corner of the window. I was going to stick my arm inside the hole from the left and try to grab him. As I put my arm inside, he practically ran into my open hand. I pulled him out and looked him over—no blood. I checked his wings and kissed him on his head. "He looks okay," I said and gave Lucas to Corky, who looked him over too.

Ray stood by Corky's side and asked, "Is there anything broken?"

"No," we told him. A man was walking by, looking at us, and he asked, "Why are y'all messing with that car?"

I told him, "We were getting our bird out the car."

"Your bird?" he said.

Corky showed him Lucas, and he stood there looking at us with an "I don't understand" look on his face as we walked away and into the building.

Back on the roof, Corky put Lucas inside the screen and locked the door. We could hear Jerry hollering, "Is he dead?"

Ray hollered back, "No."

"He's no good to me dead," yelled Jerry. All of a sudden, his brother Stanley was running to the front of his roof, chasing his birds up. Ray looked toward the open sky and saw two birds coming in our direction from the east. We watched the two birds coming closer, and Corky looked up. "Hey, that's my bird." We could see the white tips on his wings, and with him another black flight also with white tips, which might be a sister or a brother. The two black flights didn't pay any attention to Jerry's birds as they flew around their territory.

Corky hollered to Jerry and his brother, "It's my black flight coming back from vacation, and he brought back a family member. Corky was thrilled, and we were happy for him. Now he had two black flights. We couldn't wait for the two birds to land so we could have a look at his companion. Having that episode with Lucas, we forgot about the five new birds. I looked at Corky's two black flights. The other one was a girl, and one of the male birds was bugging her. Her brother wing-slapped him, and she looked just like him except she doesn't have a cap on her head. It was a beautiful summer day.

The birds welcomed Black home, and he told them, "I must speak to Sarge. I have something very important to tell him." He left his sister at the landing pad surrounded by all the female birds asking her about the east side. He found Sarge inside the coop.

He told Sarge, "The flyers from the east side are planning a stickup, a sneak attack," said Red, as he poked his head out of his cubbyhole.

"Yes," said Sarge.

The black flight continued, "They're bringing their birds into our territory."

Sarge told the nearest bird to get Rufus and Clyde. "Tell them to come here now." Then Sarge flew down from his cubbyhole. Rufus and Clyde flew into the coop, and upon hearing the story, Rufus asked when. "Soon," said the black flight.

"We must alert everyone. Start passing the words," said Sarge.

Clyde asked, "Why?"

The black flight started explaining. "Being that the bombardiers fly into their territory like it's theirs. They don't like it, and the way you three flew right through them, I must admit it was beautiful," said the black flight.

"Continue," said Sarge.

"So they figure that the bombardiers would join their birds going back to the east side."

"It's a trap," said Sarge.

"They're going to ambush us with the remaining birds that are there."

"Continue," said Sarge.

"They are tired of being showed up, so all three flyers from the east side came together and came up with this idea—a stickup."

When Sandy and Ripley and the bombardiers heard about the stickup, they did not worry because this was their territory and those guys must know there were two stocks to deal with. And when it happens, they were going to feel sorry that they came to this part of town.

Sandy was wondering how she could make me understand what was about to happen to us. I remember seeing Sandy at the trapdoor at the bottom, flapping her wings and cooing as she tried to get my attention. "I'll be right with you, sweetie," I said as I was sweeping out the holding pen, cleaning up.

Ripley flew down to Sandy and told her, "I can read your mind, Sandy. They don't need to worry about it. As long as we know, everything will be fine. As a matter of fact, Snowflake and I are looking forward to it."

Later on, as the birds were flying, we noticed Sarge heading toward the water tower and bank there. Corky told Ray, "Sarge must be getting old."

"If he keeps it up," said Ray, "I'm going to lock him up inside the holding pen for a while." Ray seemed to be a little embarrassed because he was always bragging about Sarge.

*****

Sarge sat at the water tower waiting for the crows to come, hoping he got his timing right. They usually flew across the projects going home to Jersey. He was hoping that Joe the crow was among them. He saw them coming from the east as they were yapping away.

He flew off the water tower toward them. *There's no turning back. This has to be done*, he thought.

He asked the lead crow, "Where is Joe the crow?"

"At the rear," said the crow.

Sarge flew against the incoming crows, making sure not to crash into one of them, and hollered Joe's name. "Hey, Sarge, how you doing?" said Joe the crow. Sarge flew beside him, flying over the projects, and said, "I need your help, Joe."

"How can I help you, Sarge, leader of the birds down below?" Joe winked at him.

"I need a stick about three feet long and thin enough to grab with both my claws and leave it on top of the water tower. It's really important."

"Give me some time," said Joe the crow. "I'll see what we can do for you. I hear the falcons are terrorizing this neighborhood."

"Yes, they are," said Sarge. "Joe, I must be getting back," he said as he separated himself from the pack of crows.

"Good luck with your mission," hollered Joe the crow.

Flying above the project, now approaching water tower, down went Sarge toward the roof. He didn't see Ray and he felt lucky. All the birds were wondering what Sarge was up to. As soon as he landed on the roof, he went straight into the coop. Rufus followed Sarge inside the coop. Flying into his cubbyhole with his back turned, he took a quick look at Rufus and said, "I have a mission for you. Go to Jerry's roof and tell his birds what's about to happen."

"Yes, sir." Rufus started to leave.

Sarge turned around, telling Rufus, "Sorry, my dear friend. I'm working on something that might save some lives."

"I understand," said Rufus and he flew out the coop.

*****

"What's the stickup?" asked little Joe.

"Well, that's when the competition brings their birds to your block and then let them go, hoping to pull our birds back to the east side. Ray once told me a story, there were two coops across the street from each other, and one of them lost all their birds to the other. I guess being so close to each other, I can see that happening."

It was a beautiful summer day, and I never get tired of the view from the roof. Jersey looked like it was all green, and looking downtown, I saw all the skyscrapers reaching upward. Looking straight ahead, city college buildings looked like medieval castles. Across was St. Nicholas Park, and beyond that a perfect background—beautiful blue skies.

Time went by so fast as we chased up a couple of times and watched them fly to the beat of the music coming from the radio. Ray started turning the dial on the radio and stopped at a station that was playing a waltz by Johann Strauss. I was in my own little world listening and watching Sandy and the rest of the birds flying to the waltz, no, not flying but dancing in the sky.

Corky shouted, "Change that!"

Ray told him to look up at the birds and he turned it up as far as it could go. The birds were divided into two stocks, swaying back and forth. I wished I had a movie camera. When it was all over and when they landed, we found ourselves clapping. I thought I saw Snowflake curtsy. I turned around, expecting a standing ovation from the flyers in the hood. We could see their birds flying. I knew in their hearts they knew we were the best.

Everything seemed to be so normal, and then we started hearing whistles. But it was a false alarm; it was a seagull flying high up above.

I was sitting on the wall that separated the roofs, just watching the birds. Then I noticed Sandy walking across the roof ledge. When she got to the corner of the roof, she hopped onto to the wall that I was sitting on. Sandy started walking toward me. I asked her, "What do you want, sweetie.?" She just looked at me. I noticed that she was starting to get excited she was flapping her wings up and down, and I started laughing. She seemed to be dancing to the music, now that I'm thinking about it. She was really trying to communicate with me, that they were coming—the flyers from the east side with their birds. Lots of birds.

*****

She figured if Ripley could read her mind. *Surely I could,* she thought. Nova looked at her daughter. She should've realized it by now that she was a pigeon, remembering the crush that she had on Ray. She told Ripley, who was talking to Snowflake, "Go get your sister."

Ripley replied, "Mom, can't you see that she's in love?"

"Nonsense, you're the one."

Ripley was turning red, and Snowflake asked him, "How do you know she's in love?"

"I could see the twinkle in her eyes, like the ones you have right now. That's the glare from the sun," said Ripley. He turned to look and saw that she was on his lap looking straight into his face.

*****

She got my attention, and suddenly the skylight door opened up. It was Corky coming from the store. Ray sent up a couple of sandwiches and soda. Saying I'm telling Cassondra she got competition. Sandy flew off my lap as Corky approached and gave me the sandwich and soda. She was already mad at me for spending too much time with the birds.

"She's right. You know, you're starting to look like a pigeon."

The sun was starting to set over Jersey. There was not much time left, and Corky chased up the birds, and they did too. They had been waiting for another showdown, and for a long time, we'd been getting the best of him lately. Our birds were coming from the right. It wasn't Stanley on the roof; it was his brother Jerry, and he'd been flying birds for a long time. They always chased their birds from the right as we did. This time, Jerry chased them from the left. He timed it right, as both stock blended into one in the middle of the block that separated us, going in the same direction. One big stock and the tug-of-war was starting, although it was a little different this time. They were talking, telling Jerry's birds what to expect. Hearing the sound of conga drums from the street below, as I watched, it's a beautiful sight seeing both stock flying together. They were forced into our rhythm as they circled high over our heads, and Stanley's birds started to fly off. Every bird went to their respective roof. As they landed, three birds took off again; it was Snowflake, Ripley, and Sandy.

I took a quick look toward the screen. Poor Lucas, he was locked up and watching his buddies flying. They looked like they were trying to outdo each other, but I must admit Snowflake was built for flying.

I looked up at them and saw that they were going straight up on an angle. "Snowflake's leading the way higher and higher, I wonder how high a bird can fly," said Corky. I didn't know he was standing next to me. I was so focus on the three birds. I know now a pigeon can fly as high as 6000 feet, and they kept climbing. I looked over to Jerry, and he wasn't on the roof. They made a large half circle to the right and continued going up. Corky said, "If they keep it up, there's going to be hitting pins pretty soon.

"What's hitting pins?" asked Patty.

"Yeah," said little Joe.

"It's when a bird goes up so high it looks like the head of a pin. Can you picture a head of a pin? Well, that's how high those three birds were. I mean they were up there."

"How high do you think they were?" asked little Joe.

"That's a good question. I'll estimate maybe five thousand feet."

*****

As they went higher and higher, Snowflake asked Ripley and Sandy, "How high have your ever flown?"

"This is definitely the highest for me and my sister," Ripley replied.

"It's windy up here," said Sandy. They were so high Jersey looked like a green forest. The sun was whole again; a few minutes ago, it was halfway down. "This is definitely the highest I have ever been," said Sandy, looking down between the fluffy clouds. The roof looked so small, and she saw the airport in the distance and much farther. Snowflake stopped climbing and she leveled off their gliding.

"It took some work getting up here," said Ripley.

"Isn't it beautiful?" said Snowflake as the three birds took in the view.

*****

I squinted my eyes to see if they looked like that head of a pin. "Yes, they do." Corky passed me the binoculars. I looked up, and they seemed like they were not moving. I guess they were gliding. They dipped to the right and they came down in large circles.

"I'll race you," said Sandy. About one hundred feet above the roof, they were flying in circles, corner to corner. Snowflake was leading the way, Ripley was second, and Sandy right behind him. They were streaking over the roof toward our corner and now making a turn back. No matter how hard Sandy and Ripley flew, they couldn't pass Snowflake on the opposite corner coming back. I saw Snowflake backing off and letting Ripley and Sandy pass her. Ripley slowed up and headed down to the roof, and Sandy followed. Snowflake continued flying up above.

About 150 feet up from the roof, Snowflake made a turn and started to dive down. What she did next really freaked me out—she was coming in at a steep angle, her wings tucked in. I was standing next to the landing pad looking up at her. She looked like a white missile coming in extremely fast directly at me. There couldn't be a straighter line between two points. It felt like she was taking aim at my chest. She was not slowing down, coming in at a breakneck speed. I didn't know what to make of it. It looked like she wasn't gonna stop until she hit her mark. I started jogging backward. As she reached the roof, Snowflake suddenly opened up her wings, flapping like a pigeon angel, stopping on a dime, and landing so gracefully. It was the first time one of my pigeons ever scared me, and she looked so good doing it.

I turned to look at Corky, but he was just coming out of the holding pen. "Did you see that?" His answer was "What? What did I miss?"

"It was beautiful. You should've seen it. No, I take that back."

"Why?"

I tried to describe it to Corky as best as I could. I told him, "You had to see it to believe it." I left the running part out. I noticed Sandy flying straight into the coop followed by Ripley and Snowflake. All the birds were in now. I heard the skylight door open, and it was Cassondra. Corky was inside the holding pen putting on the locks when Cassondra looked at me and told me she was not going to be home tonight. She'd been asked to go to the movies. I said, "Okay, who's taking you?"

"Jeffrey Cordero, you and your birds," she said. Then she turned away and disappeared through the skylight door.

Should I go after her? What was I going to say? I was sorry for being so slow. I guess if I really wanted her to be my girlfriend, I would've asked. I wondered why I haven't.

I watched Corky sweep the inside of the pen, thinking about the birds, especially Sand. The way she flew inside the coop, if I was not mistaken, I thought she was jealous. Maybe Cassondra was jealous of the pigeons. We finished cleaning up the roof and then went home.

When I got home, my mother wanted me to go to the store. I told her okay, and she told me that she saw me on the roof from Maria's kitchen window. "It looks like you're really enjoying yourself up there."

"Yes, I am. It's the best hobby in the world."

"You need to take a break once in a while and come home to eat."

"Corky said I'm starting to look like a pigeon." She started laughing. "If you don't come home to eat, you soon will."

*****

Inside the coop, the birds were settling in. Sandy found Ripley talking to Snowflake. She was furious in the way that Snowflake landed on the roof. Snowflake could feel the heat radiating from Sandy. Ripley said, "I think I hear my father calling," and excused himself.

"Why did you do that to him?"

"I didn't mean to scare him," said Snowflake. "I'm sorry. It's just having these wings and to be able to cut through the sky, what a wonderful feeling."

"Weren't you born with them?" Sandy being sarcastic.

"But did you see his face afterward? He was thrilled," said Snowflake. "I guess I was showing off a little bit, my darling little girl. I'm on your side. Are we still friends?"

"You will always be my friend," said Sandy. "I guess I wanted to be the one to do that to him."

"Your day will come," said Snowflake.

CHAPTER 13

The Stickup

Day 7

I couldn't wait for tomorrow to see Sandy's attitude. I woke up late and had a good breakfast. As I was walking up toward the building, I could see the birds on the ledge. We had our own individual keys.

I was trying to guess who was on the roof. I walked up the stairs past Cassondra's door and up to the skylight. I opened up the door, and it was Ray. I looked at the water can—I didn't have to go down to get some water; Ray already took care of that. We greeted each other.

He said, "Another day in the neighborhood."

"What time did you open up?" I asked.

"Eight o'clock."

I told him about what Snowflake did to me, that she scared the heck out of me, that she looked like she was going to crash into me, and that she had me running backward. He started laughing.

It was a beautiful day for flying birds; the sky was blue with some fluffy clouds in the sky. I was looking for Sandy, and she was perched on top of the skylight. As I walked toward her, she looked down on me, and I said, "Hey, sweetie, how you doing? You know you're my main girl, so don't sweat it. You're my baby, okay?" Then she flew to the edge to join the rest of the birds. I did notice Ray looking at me. "That's my girl," I told Ray.

We chased up a couple of times, and time was going by fast. We even played cornball, and he beat me, 20–18. It was now about twelve o'clock, and Stanley was on his roof with his brother. Corky walked onto the roof, and then there was sound that I dreaded, whistles being blown. We looked toward the river, and up in the sky were two falcons. I guess the guys from Riverside spotted them first. As I turned to look at our birds, twenty feet in front of the roof, I saw a lot of birds rising from the street. I thought at first there was a bunch of clinkers, but on closer examination, they were flights and grizzles. We heard Jerry chasing his birds up, and we hesitated, wondering what was going on.

Where are these birds coming from? There must've been at least over a hundred more starting to hook and swing right over the roof of my old public school across the street. They were trying to gain altitude. We ran to the edge of the roof and looked down. We saw these guys with empty boxes with a few birds remaining on the sidewalk.

Ray chased up our birds; he knew what was happening. Strange birds were in front of us, and falcons were behind us. Our birds went to the corner, making a U-turn, and we watched them as they flew in front our roof and made another right, which was strange. It looked like they wanted to clash with these birds from the East side.

The sky was full of birds, and Jerry's birds joined in, and the battle of wills was in progress. It was a surprise stickup, Ray told me about it in our many conversations about birds and trainers.

Down across the street, they started hollering, "Surprise! Surprise!" One of them hollered, "This is for your birds flying to the East side. That's our territory." He stopped talking and started looking up at his confused birds, not knowing where they were at. They needed to fly higher so they could get their bearings and see which way was home. We watched those dudes get into three cars and leave the scene of the crime, leaving empty boxes behind and maybe some birds.

We backed off the ledge and started watching the battle up above. Their birds were now trying to pull east. Jerry's birds and ours were keeping them in our territory. We backed up some more and looked upward to the sky; we knew they were not going to pull any of our birds.

I don't know about Jerry's, but we knew these birds that they brought here must've been their best birds, and now they were going back home to see the results. Waiting for your birds was half the fun; the other half was watching them land on your roof. The birds from the East side were now starting to get a sense of where they at. Some of them started to peel away from this massive gathering.

The guys from 135th were probably wondering what the heck was going on. They didn't chase their birds up because the falcons were now flying high over their roof and now heading toward us. They had a lot of birds to choose from. Sarge and the birds were aware of the falcons and it menacing presence. Jerry's birds and ours were now a super group representing our territory as they hooked and swayed back and forth. Looking up, I could only see one falcon and I wondered where the other one, it must be in the clouds.

*****

Ripley and Sandy found themselves flying with members of the dragons, telling them that his troop was in danger. "The falcons are on the hunt, and you better get on home quick."

One of the dragons from the East side was flying alongside Snowflake, mimicking every move she made. She turned and said, "You're good. I like your style."

"What's your name?" he asked her.

"Snowflake…and yours?"

"Arial."

"Have you noticed that falcon up above?"

"I am not blind," he said. "There is safety in numbers, and there are a lot of birds to choose from."

"Arial, most of your friends are leaving, and by the way, why are you here?"

"We were hoping to take some of you back with us. Our trainers from the East side are jealous of you. They see you every day coming into our territory, ripping away from your home like you're homing pigeons. And deep in their hearts, they wish that they had a stock like yours."

"Thank you. We know we're good," she replied.

"Looking at her, he rolled his eyes. "Modest, aren't you?"

More birds were peeling off in bunches and heading straight home toward the east. The falcon was high above them, and he had his eyes on them.

This huge stock made a right high above the school before starting to divide. Jerry's birds went to their roof, and Snowflake told Arial, "Why don't you stick around a little bit longer until the danger's over? The falcon is following your friends. He has killed two birds already."

"I think I will," said Arial. "Not because of the falcon but because of you."

"Yeah, right," she said. "I have a boyfriend. His name is Ripley."

*****

Ray was looking through the binoculars and giving us a blow-by-blow of what he was seeing. I looked up; it almost looked like a tornado of birds. The birds from the east side were being whipped out of the funnel, heading home. Our birds seemed to calm down.

They started to fly their normal pattern. The rest of Jerry's birds were going home. Our birds were descending upon the roof, and I looked for Sandy. I spotted Snowflake flying with Ripley, and Sandy was with them. We backed up away from the ledge, not to scare any strays that would be landing on the roof.

As they landed, we could see a bunch of new birds by the color of their band. They weren't Jerry's birds, as he flew blue bands. I saw three different color bands—white, black, and purple—and the birds had their eyes on the falcon that was flying high above us.

Looking toward Jerry's roof, I saw the brothers were pretty busy trying to catch the strays that landed on their roof. Looking up at the falcon, I guess there were too many birds. It couldn't make up his mind which one to get, or maybe it was not in a hurry. I started looking our birds over to make sure we didn't lose any. As I was doing that, Corky was setting up the traps. Lucas was inside the screen and he flew out. I saw Sandy looking at me, and we made eye contact. I never had a bird like Sandy before. It was like I wanted to take her home to meet my mother.

Now to catch these strays from the east side, Ray threw some food, trying to lead them to the trapdoor. Some of our birds came down to eat, and some of the strays followed them. Ray cleverly separated the stray from our birds closer to the trapdoor at the bottom. We managed to catch a few using the trapdoor, and we picked off a few when they went to drink, and the ones that were watching stood away from the water can and the roof floor.

We noticed on the ledge a blue flight from the east side had the hots for Snowflake. He was doing his courtship dance, bopping his head up and down and going around in little circles and spreading his tail feathers like a fan in a sweeping motion.

He was neither hungry or thirsty; he had his eyes on Snowflake. We noticed Ripley flying toward the landing pad, and he landed between Snowflake and the blue flight. All of a sudden, there was a fierce battle going on as they tried to push each other off the roof. The blue flight wing slapped Ripley, who quickly returned one of his own. They were breast-to-breast pecking at each other. I heard Corky and Ray rooting for Ripley.

Ripley pushed the blue flight to the edge and knocked him off the roof. The blue flight flew to the end of the landing pad. I noticed Ripley started doing his courtship dance; his head kept bobbing up and down and his tail feathers in a sweeping motion, opening up wide and closing and opening again. Snowflake was impressed, but she turned her back. Then she asked Ripley, "What took you so long?"

He replied, "Well, I had a little trouble with my steps. She slowly turned and joined him. He was mesmerized by her movements, and they were bugging beautifully together as the music played on the radio. He was now letting all the males know that Snowflake was his. They started kissing, and the courtship was sealed.

Sandy happened to be at the other end of the roof where the blue flight landed. He started his courtship dance on Sandy, and she quickly wing-slapped him across his face and took off and landed on my shoulder. Corky told Ray, "Have you ever seen anything like that? That bird is in love with you, dude."

I started mimicking the noise the males do, and doing the bug dance with Sandy on my shoulder. She poked me in the ear with her beak and flew off to the top of the pigeon coop. Corky and Ray were laughing their heads off.

After the laughter wore off, now our attention was on the falcons. All the flyers in the hood were watching the falcons crossing the river and probably wondering where the other one. Corky looked through the binoculars and spotted the other falcon in the cloud. We saw it going in and out of the clouds, and then it started to dive down to its mate. The speed that he used to reach the falcon down below was amazing. They were now flying toward Jersey. From what I knew, the female was always larger than the male. You could almost hear them squawking at each other as they continued on their way. It was safe again.

We heard noise coming from above and we turned our heads and saw a bunch of crows coming from who knows where. Sarge flew to the ledge. The crows were now flying over my building, and one decided to land on the water tower, and they all did. I thought the birds didn't seem to be agitated by the crows. If they just stopped yapping, "Her, her, her." But it didn't last long, as they started taking off toward Jersey.

We heard Jerry and Stanley calling our names, asking what was that about, I told them they must be mad something. Jerry shouted out, "Your birds keep ripping in that direction and teasing them. Now you have to return the favor you have to tag them back, and if you don't, you have to forfeit fifty birds." I told Jerry his birds were involved, too, and he said, "The stickup was a challenge against you."

"Isn't it supposed to be twenty," Ray shouted.

"I guess y'all didn't see the memo on the bulletin board at Mike pet shop." We walked over to the corner building so we didn't have to shout at each other. Both brothers walked over three roofs. We were now across the street from each other. Ray told him, "We didn't agree to any of that stuff."

"It doesn't matter," said Jerry.

"Stop joking around!" Corky said. "Have Mike's number at the pet shop. He will verify it. I guess that's what happened when you buy fifty pounds bag of pigeon feed."

Not once did we visit the pet shop during the winter. "It doesn't matter," Ray said. "We're not giving up fifty birds. I guess we have to play tag."

Jerry told us he'd give us a box of his best birds when we were ready to tag them up, which was pretty cool of him.

"That sounds great," Ray said. "We going to need all the help we can get. There are three stocks down there."

Stanley said, "I think those are the guys in the middle. Your birds better bring our birds back.

Ray told him, "Don't worry. We be bringing more than your birds back." Ray turned to the brothers. "And by the way, how many strays did you catch?"

"Three," they answered with big smile on their faces.

"We'll let you know when we're ready." Ray tried to play it off like it was no big deal, but I could see a worried look on Ray's face.

Ray asked Corky, "What's wrong with Lucas?" I told Ray that he was mad at Corky for locking him up. "How do you know?" he asked me.

I started boasting. "Not only do I fly birds, but I also study them. He hasn't tumbled right."

Corky's reply was, "Maybe that visit to the street knocked it out of him. I should be mad at him for almost killing himself." That was Corky's answer to that.

As time went by, I was looking at our birds flying and I felt proud at the way they handled the adversities that were being thrown at them. Ray looked up at the birds and said, "It looks like those two new birds from the east side found themselves a new home."

We noticed Sarge flying away from the stock and heading toward the water tower. Sure enough, he banked on the water tower. Corky told Ray, "Sarge must be getting old."

Ray said, "I told you if he does it again, I was going to lock him up."

I picked up the binoculars and looked at the Dutchman birds flying. Then I looked toward the east side. "Hey, fellas, I see about ten birds flying near Seventh Avenue near 125th Street. I think someone's trying to start up a new stock."

"We see them," Ray said.

Corky said more competition, the more the merrier, I said, those guys probably lost that white tipplet.

Ray said, "More strays for us."

I passed the binoculars to Ray. "Welcome to falcon land," said Ray as he looked through the binoculars in the background towards the east side. He noticed that one stock was ranging out of their territory.

*****

Sarge was walking to the back of the water tower; he was looking for his stick. And there it was, about twenty-four inches long and skinny. He wrapped his claws around it to get a feel for it. He started flapping his wings, rising up a few inches and thinking to himself, *We can do this.* But he was hoping that the wind didn't change directions and knock it off the water tower and onto the street. He turned the stick in the direction of the wind, hoping the wind didn't change.

He flew off the water tower and headed for the roof and caught up with his friends. Sarge told Rufus the bombardiers were no longer grounded. He ripped away from the stock and headed down. Ray was about to leave when he saw Sarge coming. "You better get your butt down here." He was waiting for Sarge to hit the roof so he could tell him he was grounded. Sarge was on the landing pad. Ray walked up to Sarge and asked him, "What's wrong with you?" Ray turned, looking at me, and said, "Now you got me talking to the birds." He didn't try to lock up Sarge. "If he does it again, fellas, make sure to tell me."

Corky told Ray to wait up and that he was leaving too.

Ray said, "Hey, rookie, do you need help locking up?"

"Did you say 'rookie'? Man, I am the captain of the all-star team. You looking at one bad pigeon, dude. I'll see you guys later."

I liked being alone with the birds. I wasn't alone too long; Peewee came through the door straight toward me, sniffing and jumping on me. His tail was constantly smacking my leg. The birds were about to hit the roof when Peewee started barking at them. They started going back up again, and I watched them as they rose higher. Lucas had yet to tumble. I saw Jerry's birds landing on their roof. There was just about two hours flying time left before the sun went down.

Looking up, I noticed the bombardiers were itching for a rip, and there they went. I picked up the binoculars and started tracking them as the rest of the stock were circling the roof, coming down slowly. Going forward were Ripley, Sandy, Snowflake, Lucas, Corky's two black flights Vicki and Penny, Charlie, and another Canadian.

"Who's the blower of that whistle?" I saw Jerry blowing his whistle.

CHAPTER 14

The Falcons Are Hungry

This is what a typical flight looks like. They come in many colors. What distinguishes them from the rest is their pink beak, and the wing tips are usually white. He is standing on top of a water can.

Once inside the coop, Sarge told Rufus and Clyde to follow him, and with their flapping wings, they did. They followed him up to his cubbyhole. He started pointing to a diagram on the wall. It was a long stick. Clyde asked him, "Is this the reason you've been spending so much time by yourself? The falcons are hovering over our territory, and the young bombardiers are out there, and this is your secret weapon?"

Rufus interrupted, "I am not praying to no stick. Have you lost your mind?"

"No, no," said Sarge, trying to explain. "Look what happens when I do this." He drew a bird with his wings extended from its side straight out and clutching the stick with his claws. Then Sarge added four more birds with their wings overlapping each other.

Sarge continued with his battle plan. "What we need is two strong flights to carry the weight of the other birds on the stick, and the flights will have to fly in unison."

"Two wings and a prayer," said Rufus.

Clyde asked him, "Why?"

"Because the only thing falcons are scared of is a bird bigger than them. I call it Mission Condor," said Sarge.

"And where are we gonna find such a stick?" asked Clyde.

"On the water tower," answered Sarge. "Joe the crow brought me the perfect stick."

"So that's what you been up to," said Rufus. Sarge continued with his illustration on the wall. "All we have to do is jump off the water tower together and glide and then we will be one big bird."

One of the birds hollered, "Falcon up above!" They all looked at one another. Sarge leaped from his cubbyhole, and his two friends followed straight out the coop and right through the trapdoors onto the roof floor. Looking up, Sarge said, "It's Ramses and Karzai."

"You know these falcons?" asked Clyde.

"No, I only know their names. The female is the meanest."

*****

I heard Ray whistling; he had this funny way of whistling. I looked over the edge and saw the word *love* painted on top of a moving truck a building over. I saw Ray on the corner pointing upward to the sky. He saw the falcons flying overhead, and I hollered back, "Birds ripping!" I also noticed people gathered, looking up toward the sky. The falcons were in full view.

The birds on the landing pad looked anxious; half of the stock were flying into the coop. Most of the parents on the landing pad looked up, and so did I, hoping not to see the young bombardiers. No such luck. I could see them far off in the distance now flying above a fluffy cloud; they were coming home. *That's not good.* I picked up the binoculars, looking at the falcons. They were flying underneath the same cloud. *What can I do to let them know that the falcons are underneath them?* I picked up the whistle that was on top of the coop and looked up. I started blowing hard and loud, and the birds on the ledge quickly went up and came right back down. I was hoping that the young bombardiers could make the connection—whistle meant falcon. Sarge, Clyde, and Rufus flew to the top of the coop, and Sarge told Rufus, "Find me two strong flights and tell them what we plan to do."

Rufus flew into the screen and went inside the coop. I could hear Jerry blowing his whistle too. I appreciated his help. Inside the coop, Rufus was asking for volunteers. Without hesitation, the blue flight from the East side walked over to Rufus's side. Rufus looked around for one more, and the yellow flight flew down to Rufus's side. "So let's do this," said the yellow flight.

Up in the sky high above the roof, the bombardiers heard the whistles. Looking down, they saw the falcons between the clouds below.

Ripley, with Snowflake by his side and Sandy up above him and Lucas to his left, told the bombardiers to tighten up as he led them toward the east and away from our territory.

I was looking through the binoculars and I could see the birds were flying away from danger; I was relieved. I heard the skylight door open I turned and saw that it was Ray. I told him we were in trouble.

"I know," he said and asked me for the binoculars and started tracking the bombardiers headed toward the east. "Those damn falcons," he said, looking toward the pigeon coop and seeing three birds flying out and onto the top of the pigeon coop. He saw Sarge there with four other birds.

*****

Sarge told his war birds, "When I say go, shoot straight for the water tower. Did you explain to them what we were doing, Rufus?"

"Yes," he answered. "They are ready."

*****

Tracking the bombardiers, Ray and I saw the stocks from the East side up in the air. The falcons were now flying much higher than before. They must've spotted the bombardiers flying away from them. All we could do now was to wait and see what happens.

Unaware to us, the traffic on Amsterdam Avenue had stopped. People were stepping out of their cars, and the people on the buses were wondering why everyone was pointing toward the sky. Curiosity got the best of them. Within a few seconds, the bus was empty. People were pouring into the park for better views.

*****

Ripley decided to fly away from the east side and circle back as he saw the three stocks flying over their territory. To his right, he could see the East River. Ripley was trying to formulate a plan on how to get the bombardiers down on the roof. He had to think fast; the sun was going down over Jersey. Lucas told Ripley, "Maybe we should come in low."

Ripley replied, "No, the falcons will jump them from above. We have to stay high and make a dive for home."

Snowflake suggested that they should divide into two groups and come in from two different directions. "This will probably confuse the falcons. It sounds good, but we will stick together," Ripley told her. They were flying at a fast pace, and Sandy told Ripley to slow down. "We must conserve our energy for what lies ahead," she said, and Ripley agreed. They slowed down a bit. Ripley thought about what Rufus told them—that a falcon can reach the speed of two hundred miles per hour in a steep dive. They would have to use all the skills that they learned in their young lives. Ripley saw a worried look on his sister's face. "Don't worry, sis. We'll make it." Corky's two black flights, Black and his sister, were among them.

Black suggested that they should land on one of the roofs on the east side. At least, it would be safe and they could come back when they were released. Upon hearing this, Snowflake replied, "I am not drinking water out of no foreign water can." Ripley started laughing, and they all did, too, which was a relief for now. She told him, "We are the bombardiers and we do not get caught." Lucas added, "And we don't surrender." So with that said, they headed home. Sandy was looking toward the west, and she could see the water tower, saying to herself, "Home." She wanted to see her parents and D's face again.

*****

On the roof, Ray was telling me that the bombardiers were flying high and coming straight toward us. I asked for the binoculars and started looking. I could see they bunched up in a tight group and were coming straight home. I lifted the binoculars and saw the falcons flying between the clouds and then disappearing.

*****

On top of pigeon coop, Sarge was getting ready, and Clyde told Sarge, "I see the bombardiers."

Sarge said, "Wait until the falcons are in the clouds" Clyde thought about Ripley and Sandy. Sarge had his cloud cover and said, "Let's go."

Rufus hollered, "Fly fast, fly hard, fly higher," and they leapt forward. Sarge led the way toward the water tower straight up they flew. Ray and I turned around, hearing the flapping of wings, and saw Sarge leading the birds toward the water tower. Ray shouted at them, this is no time for banking, they landed, we don't see them. What you mean by banking, asked David, it's an analogy for a bank manager who sits all day.

They flew onto the water tower. Sarge started looking for the stick, but it was not where he left it. The wind must have blown it off.

"Where is this stick?" said Sarge, trying not to panic.

"Maybe it flew off onto the street," one of the birds said. The blue flight hollered, "There's the stick on the roof."

Sarge told Clyde to follow him, and they landed on the roof. Each took one end of the stick with the claws and lifted the stick to the water tower. They got in position—Sarge in the middle, Rufus on his left, and Clyde to his right—and they interlocked their wings, the blue flight at the left and the yellow flight at the right.

Sarge said, "Whatever happens, do not let go of the stick," thinking he wished he had more time to see if this would work. Together they leapt forward, and the wind pushed them backward like a kite with no strings. The flights strained to give them lift, flying against the wind. Sarge hollered, "Fly with the wind!" as they turned and picked up speed, trying to find updrafts. Then they felt the warm air pushing them up higher and higher, and they were now leveled with the clouds.

The young bombardiers flying across Manhattan were heading home. "Where did these clouds come from?" asked Sandy. Ripley was heading up, and the rest followed. They were flying high between two cumulus clouds, and there were some more up ahead. Ripley told the bombardiers that they were going to dive through the clouds and straight down to the roof. Snowflake, looking straight ahead, was surprised to see the two falcons hovering over the clouds and blocking their way home.

The bombardiers noticed another big bird behind the falcons gliding near their territory. This one was bigger than the falcons. What an ugly-looking bird. Snowflake caught up with Ripley and heard him whispering, "We're not going to make it."

"Ripley, we are going to make it. A true bombardier never gives up hope."

"Incoming straight ahead," said Lucas. Ramses flew toward them, which sent a chill through the bombardiers. They couldn't take their eyes off Ramses as he was getting larger. They were underestimating his speed. The bombardiers were set up like bowling pins; Ramses was the bowling ball. At the point of impact reaching with his large claws, his large wingspan spread out. Ripley turned vertical swinging to the right, and Snowflake also went vertical diving to the left. Half of the bombardiers followed Ripley, and the other half followed Snowflake. Ramses was going so fast he flew straight between them, reaching out with his claws as he went by.

Ripley quickly noticed that Snowflake and Sandy were no longer with him. They separated by one hundred feet or more. The falcon was making a U-turn and was now going after Ripley and his little gang.

Sarge trying to time his attack. "Down, boys," he ordered, flying between the clouds. "Hold the line, I mean the stick."

Keziah hovered between two clouds, her eyes on Snowflake's group coming closer. To her right, she saw five birds racing for home, Ramses about thirty yards behind them in hot pursuit. Ripley took a quick look up to the right, and gliding above the clouds was that strange-looking bird. *How did Rufus fail to tell us about this one, which was so terrifying to look at?* It pushed Ripley into a decision knowing that the big bird would probably jump them before they reached the roof. Ripley decided to take the bombardiers under the cloud and then straight down, hoping they could pick up enough speed going down and avoid being snatched by one of the predators.

Sandy looked to her left and saw her brother with his group going under the clouds; with him were the two black flights. She looked to the right, and there was Lucas with a determined look on his face now winking at her.

Snowflake was in front leading her small group of bombardiers. The falcon put a big wedge between them. Ramses was gaining on Ripley's group. Snowflake shouted, "Head for the clouds!" There was one right in front of them. "And once in, make a right turn and fly straight down to the roof as fast as you can and bring your wings in as tight as possible." *So that's how she does it*, Sandy thought. Underneath them every roof looked the same as they passed by, from gray to green and now flying over St. Nicholas Park. She saw the Dutchman's roof to the right.

Keizah flapped her wings in the distance. She suddenly made her move, leaping toward them from up above.

"We must reach the cloud before contact," said Lucas.

Sandy hollered, "Fly hard, fly faster—" Nothing else came out. Bingo—above was the falcon streaking downward. Sandy told him, "Don't look at it."

Snowflake yelled, "Keep your eyes on the cloud."

The falcon was getting larger. They could hear noise coming off her wings. The bombardiers were five seconds faster than the falcon. They just made it into the clouds, and in the cloud passing over their heads, heading down behind them was this dark shadow. They made a right going home.

It was quiet in the cloud. "Stick together," said Snowflake in a low tone. They could barely hear their wings flapping. Sandy watched Snowflake disappear and reappear against the background of the clouds. Down below Ripley and his group were flying as fast as they could. They had their eyes on the roof and were heading straight down from beneath the cloud.

That crazy-looking bird was coming out into the open, and Ripley didn't want to look at it. Ramses was about ten feet behind Ripley's group and coming in fast. Ramses suddenly stopped its pursuit; these big ugly birds distracted him, and it seemed to be coming right at him. Ramsey took a quick look at Ripley's group getting away.

Ripley hollered, "Fly hard, fly farther, fly fast," and down they went, hearing sweeping sounds coming off their wings as the roof was getting larger and larger. Ripley could see D and Ray on the roof, and they were coming down like little jet planes. Ripley could hear and see D and Ray cheering and jumping for them as they landed on the roof.

Ripley and the birds landed, but Sandy and Snowflake weren't among them. Nova flew over to Ripley and asked him about his sister. "She's with Snowflake," he replied.

"Your father and Sarge and Rufus are up there too. That big bird you saw was them."

"How can that be?" asked Ripley.

"I will explain it to you later," said Nova as both of them turned their heads to the sky. It was almost certain that all the flyers in the hood were watching this unfold.

Flying through the silent clouds, Snowflake saw an opening directly ahead, right over the roof. When they reached the opening, they started pouring out of the bottom of the clouds, coming straight down. Karzai was waiting down below. On the roof, I was hollering, "Go back into the clouds! Go back." But it was too late; they were committed to their plan.

Sandy slowed down; the sight of the falcon terrified her. The falcon turned its head from right to left as Snowflake and the bombardiers shot right past her. Sandy couldn't take her eyes off Karzai. Such a beautiful bird. Now she was turning to Mr. Gray, realizing she was the last bird going down. She was scared that Karzai would cut her off on a way to the roof. She flew up into the cloud.

Above the clouds, Sarge Condor was working fine. He said, "I am the head. The flights are my wings. The condor lives again." The falcon below looked up and braced himself for a battle; it was

Ramses. Sarge did not want to get too close, hoping to scare him enough to fly away. "Pull your heads in fellas." Before he realized this bird had five heads.

"Well, maybe that will scare him away," said Clyde.

Sarge said, "Let's keep his attention on us." He barked out orders—tales up would make them go up; tales down would make them dip down. He tried to make them look mean and threatening as much as possible, and Clyde wondered what was happening below.

*****

On the roof, Ray and I were watching the birds coming down. I could see Snowflake leading the way, flying directly at the falcon, which looked confused. I saw my little white stallion coming down like a white missile with the rest of the birds trailing behind her, mimicking her every move. I heard cars blowing their horns down below. I could hear cheers and hollers coming from the streets.

"She's bringing them down," I heard Ray say with great pleasure. "Come on, baby, bring them home! Did you see that?" They flew right past the falcon. "Damn, that bird is good."

She was coming down in the same angle that she used when she had me jogging backward. If she didn't slow down, they would crash on the roof. She pulled up just in time at the edge of the landing pad with her beautiful self, and the rest followed. I could see Sandy was not one of them. "Sandy is missing!"

Ray told me, "I saw a bird ducking into the clouds. It has to be her."

I couldn't believe that Sandy was up there by herself, somewhere in the clouds. I walked over to the ledge to take a look down below and saw people on the sidewalk looking up. The traffic had stopped going both ways; they were there standing beside their cars, looking up. People were in the park across the street, some of them pointing up with their fingers. I saw people stepping off the bus and looking up at the falcon. I called out to Ray to come, and he took a look down below and saw his boss on the corner looking up too. I backed off the ledge and looked up at the clouds to see if I could find Sandy.

Now I saw what appeared to be a dark floating rag coming out of the clouds.

Ray was looking through the binoculars. "What the heck?" he said in a loud voice.

"Is it a floating rag?" I asked.

"If it is, it has wings."

"Stop jiving," I told him. Ray passed me the binoculars, and I heard him say, "I've never seen anything like that in my life." As I looked through the binoculars, this flying thing disappeared into the clouds. I pointed the binoculars on the water tower and saw that Sarge and the birds were gone. The sun was no longer shining, and the clouds were getting dark and menacing.

All the pigeons had their eyes to the sky. I took a quick look at the landing pad and saw Ripley and Snowflake and Nova.

*****

Snowflake was telling Ripley, "Whatever you do, do not leave this roof," as she turned and flew to the back of the roof, which no one noticed.

Up above the clouds, Sarge turned his condor to the right, looking down on Ramsey, who was about twenty feet away. Ramses was looking up ready for a fight, and slowly flapping his wings with his claws extended outward. All of a sudden, Sandy popped up from beneath a cloud. Clyde seeing his daughter, he whispered her name, Sarge trying to position his Condor between Sandy and Ramses. He caught a glimpse of the other falcon, Karzai, hovering beneath them.

The falcons needed to make one more kill before the sun went down; the youngsters were hungry. Up above Ramses looked confused. Sarge decided to go after Karzai. *Surely if she flies away, Ramses is sure to follow*, he thought.

The flights at both end of the stick looked at Sarge's movement of his head; they knew which way to go. So down they went, leaving Ramsey fluttering in midair.

Meanwhile, Sandy was flying through the clouds, realizing that water vapors were starting to soak her wings. She could feel the coldness and the added weight as she flew out of one cloud and into another. Sandy caught a glimpse of a long flying wing as it disappeared in the cloud above her and wondered what that could be. Now she saw Karzai between the clouds below, circling. Sandy's instinct told her to stay in the cloud, but she was getting soaked. She didn't want to get caught out in the open with wet wings, but she knew she had to make a run for home. She flew inside a cloud surrounded by fog, and suddenly Snowflake was flying next to her.

Snowflake disappeared and reappeared and told Sandy, "By the power of Zeus, I grant you your wish. Your destiny awaits you. Just do what you have to do. Bless you, my child." Sandy blinked and Snowflake disappeared. The fear she was feeling got her seeing things. She flew down, skimming the bottom of a fluffy cloud. "I want to go home." Sandy noticed that the roof was behind her—she was flying away from home; she had to turn around. As she was making the turn, Karzai saw Sandy and she wondered, *Where is Ramses? He should be flushing this pigeon out of the clouds.* Sandy flew back in the cloud after seeing Karzai.

*****

Down on the roof, I could hear Jerry's saying, "It's gonna get your pigeon."

*****

Karzai entered the fluffy cloud to intercept Sandy, hoping to be there waiting for this smart little pigeon.

Sarge dove into the clouds, leaving Ramses flapping his wings there. Then Karzai noticed a large dark figure with a large wingspan hovering in the cloud. Right there and then, Sandy flew right past her, and Karzai kept her eyes on this bird that was getting closer and larger by the second. She made a turn; induced by the thought of her two youngsters, she thought could not risk being injured. But it was the wrong turn, which would lead into a collision course with the condor. Sarge, giving direction with his head and neck, didn't realize the flights were having a hard time seeing him through the mist.

He pointed upward with his head, but they kept going down. and Keizai, she didn't see the Condor bearing down on her, the end of the stick hit Keizai head,' the birds on the stick were horrified. Karzai was stunned and slightly dizzy by the blow upside her head. Thinking that this crazy-looking bird wanted to eat her, she hightailed it out of there, heading toward Jersey.

Sandy thought that these two big birds were behind her, and she decided to go for it. As soon as she jumped out the cloud, there was Ramses watching his mate leave; it was up to him to bring the food home. Sandy found herself above the clouds, desperately trying to think of a plan.

"Don't panic," said the spider, "and don't let fear cloud your judgment." All of a sudden, she felt the warmness of the sun rays drying her feathers. She circled the cloud one more time, absorbing the sunrays. Now there was a beautiful sunset over Jersey, and she saw a rainbow for the first time. *How beautiful*, she thought. A calmness came over her, and she was no longer scared. Looking down between the clouds, she caught a glimpse of the top of the water tower down below. She tilted her wings to the left and, headfirst, dove down below. She was flying between the clouds, flapping and tucking her wings in tight. There was a powerful downdraft of cold air rushing between the two clouds, which was making her go as twice as fast as she ever flew before, which gave her confidence.

*****

Up on the roof I'm hearing a haunting melody coming from the radio. Seeing Sandy jettisoned out between the clouds, and my heart was racing. Ramses saw Sandy, and thinking this might be the last chance to bring the food home, he went after her. In a great burst of speed, he had Sandy in his crosshairs.

Sandy spotted him up above, and she started to take evasive action, as he was coming down on her fast. She heard a sweeping sound coming off his wings, and she started rolling to the right. Ramses rolled to the right, mimicking her every move and going down like a corkscrew. Ramses, with his large wings tucked in, came in fast. Sandy twisted to the left, and Ramses twisted to the left, following her every move. *This pigeon is fast*, he thought, *but not as fast as me.* Sandy's circle was getting smaller and smaller, and she was beginning to twirl like a top, her eyelids fluttering. My heart was pounding. I felt like I was floating upward. There was no roof, but I felt the roof under my feet. There was no Ray; I saw nothing, just Sandy. I could see the falcon breathing down her back.

*****

Sandy was thinking of Rufus's lesson down in the basement about inverted loops, which were only to be done in case of emergency and this was definitely one. She was going down too fast, but it didn't really matter. She opened up her wings, just enough to slow her down. She felt the strain on her wings as she broke out of the dive, pushing her tail feathers up. She heard a swishing sound, and it was getting louder; he was closing in on her. As Sandy curved upward, Ramses shot right past her, missing her by a couple of inches. Sandy went upward, flapping her wings as fast as she could, and went straight up; she must complete the loop. Up and over she went, and the world was upside down. She saw Ramses was looping, too, but his was much larger.

*****

On her back, a patch of blue sky. She completed the loop and down she went, while Ramses was looping, he lost sight of her. There she was down below; the gap had widened. The roof was coming at her, she sees D with his arm extended upwards, sanctuary she thought sanctuary, but is arms are not long enough and then a loud' thump, feathers, feathers floating from the impact, I screamed out no…

Now I hear the screams and moans coming from the street like the roar of the crowd at a stadium as the falcon snatched her out of the sky, he is now trying to squeeze the life out of her, thunderclaps.

The Condor trying to catch up with Ramses, Clyde letting go of the stick streaking downwards he caught up with the falcon and jumped him from the back behind him was Sarge and Rufus joining in, scratching at Ramses with their little tiny claws, the two flights did not want no part of this rumble.

Startled by their actions Ramsey had to let go of Sandy, to fend off these crazy birds, but she's not flying.

She was dropping straight down, thunderclaps' she was dropping two roofs over, I had my eyes on her', I jumped over to the next roof and ran across and leaped over the small wall, as she was about to hit the floor I reached out, I caught her' as I slid on my knees, it started to rain as I held her lifeless body in my hands, I started to give her mouth to beak resuscitation as my tears started coming down.

It felt like my little world was crying with me, as the rain God letting go of their tears, on the third floor fire escape a girl in a pony-tail is looking up at the drama that's unfolding in front of her from her new apartment. She seems to be in a trans-her grandmother sticking her head out the window telling Candida to come inside before she gets an attack of asthma. Candida is telling her grandmother that she saw an angel in the clouds it seemed to be speaking to her, as she entered the apartment through the window.

The Grandmother asked what did this angel say, that's funny I don't remember now. Candida hugs her grandmother telling her that she doesn't have asthma anymore, what do you mean, it's gone', desperately' wanting to believe her granddaughter. Letting go of her grandmother, and starts running towards the front door, where you going child' someone is upstairs waiting for me. 'who "waiting for you,' ask the grandmother.

The roof is pulsating like a rapid heartbeat, now there's a low humming sound in my ear. What's happening to me? Looking up the clouds are dark and mean looking, the rumbling sound of thunder, the skylight door opens, with watery eyes, I see a pretty girl with a ponytail tied in a yellow ribbon, standing there, in blue jeans with a pink sweater, her arm holding the door open, as the rain drops were falling, she's getting wet', she's looking at me, l don't recognize her, letting go of the door.

She's walking towards me, she getting drenched, I started to get up, but she kneels down beside me, and put her arm around my shoulders, in a sweet calming voice' asking me, was that your pigeon, yes, it was. She said, I can see that you truly loved her. How does she know it's a her', I thought to myself. Whatever is happening on this roof it's only happening' to me'. I can smell the sweet scent of Wrigley's gum on her breath. The humming is back, I see her lips moving, as the skylight door opens again, I turned to look, an elderly' lady, motioning' to her', to come in from the rain. I see the lady lips moving, as lightning struck the water tower' with a big bang', I saw the old lady body jerk. On my roof I can hear Ray running for the skylight. I can hear again, Candida, come in now! Screamed the old lady.

The humming sound is back, as I held Sandy between my hands seeing the yellow band on her tiny leg. Candida put her hands on top of the Sandy lifeless body. Another white flash across' the sky' followed by a bang our body jerk. As the rain continued to fall. All of a sudden I'm feeling a heartbeat between my hand, Sandy is wiggling.

Candida took her hands off of Sandy. Sandy standing up in my hands, as she launches herself up, flapping her wings flying' over my head towards our roof, dropping a calling card on my thigh. Candida laugh, I would never have done that to you, I'm stung' what

As she was getting up, she plucked me in my ear with her finger, remembering Sandy pecking' me in the same spot. I looked up at her, the rain is subsiding, she gave me a beautiful smile, she's looking towards my roof, you have a beautiful coop, looking at her the rain drops on her face' makes her look like she was crying. She has a fair complexion and pretty, looking into her brown eyes, I'm Candida' but my friends call me candy. I'm asking her' do you believe in love at first sight, I can't believe I said that I'm sorry. Yes I do believe', I have this strange feeling that I know you Danny, how do you know my name, I must've heard it down in the street', while I was on my fire escape' she said.

The rain has suddenly stopped. We both looked up at the clouds, they're starting to part' sunrays are starting to appear between the clouds, she's asking me, may I come up and visit you and your pigeons, telling her she could come up anytime she wants. Thinking to myself after' what she did' of course. I got off my knees. She slowly started to walk away, then she turned around looking at me, we're both the same, you and I, how 'I asked, she said we both don't have enough sense' to come in out of the rain. As she turned walking towards the skylight dripping wet, as the sunrays seem to follow her.

She gave me one last look, as the old lady held the door open, she seems to float into the skylight. The old lady waved at me as the door is closing I can hear her saying what's wrong with you girl, in Spanish. I started singing it's just my imagination running away with me. Ray was by my side by now, saying it's a good thing you caught Sandy before she hit the roof. The falcon didn't win this one Ray, he started patting me on my back. I'm still wondering what's going on. Then he asked me who was that girl. I am looking towards my building on the 11th floor window I think I see my mother with her friends looking at me. I waved at them letting them know I'm okay. I'm telling Ray, you won't believe me if I told' you, wiping my tears away, come on man' I'll believe' you' he said. I told him no...' Remembering the card trick on the night of the blackout, wiping my tears away above the roof In 3-D. Come on tell me.

Across the street my mother is looking out the window with her two friends Maria, and Doris, tears running down my mother's cheek. As she sang a Spanish song she used to sing to me as a kid, her friends singing along with her as she saw me recklessly leaping from roof to roof desperately trying to catch my beloved Sandy before she hit the roof. Singing coocoo roo coo cooo...paloma, don't cry my beautiful pigeon.

Up above Athena sitting on the clouds with her legs dangling looking down at her creation, hearing the voice from above, its Zeus, telling her, I did not send you down there to stir the pot, but you did well everyone up here is pleased, thank you my Lord, we're also pleased with Haytheus performance he made it interesting, Athena turns around you can come out the clouds now, I know you there', he's becoming visible to the eye, don't you know love always wins at the end. You were very clever, but it's not over yet' Athena', there's still a game of tag" that must be played". Are you up to it, The voice from the heavens, saying both of your come on home now'.

Looking up towards the clouds, as I finish telling my story, the thought of my Buddy came to mine, I better get moving, and I have to help Miss Maggie with her groceries, kids I gotta go. That was an amazing story said Patty. It sounds like a neat hobby said little Joe, asking was Lucas real, yes he was real, the best tumbler in the world. Did you really find Lucas inside the car' asked David, yes 'we found him in the car?

Patty is looking at me with a smile, there's one question' Mr. D that the fellas obviously forgot to ask, was Candida real' or was she part of the magic' show. Candida was real all right, Candida and I been together ever since.

You don't say', said Patty so it really was magic. Do you want to see a picture of us together. Yes, said Patty, the boys shaking their heads up and down in agreement, the picture is pretty old it was taken about 25 years ago, digging inside my wallet. As they stood up, I handed Patty the picture, she's beautiful 'said Patty, you were in dreads Mr. D, she looks like a Sandy' said David. Patty asking the boys, Doesn't she' looks like a pretty pigeon, yup' said little Joe.

David asking, Did you really hear the humming sound and the heartbeat on the roof. Well', I had' to make the story 'interesting, You sure did' a good job' said Patty.

Handed me back my picture. Getting up heading towards the skylight door. What happened to Sandy shouted' Patty. I turned around to look at them, little David is looking toward the open sky. That's another story which I don't have time to tell you. Little Joe is asking do the pet shop on the east side still sell birds, I don't know. Opening up the skylight door getting ready to go in, hearing little Joe saying come back soon' and finished the story, yeah said Patty, and help us build a little pigeon coop. I turned around looking at them, I might' just do that. Walking into the skylight and headed downstairs on the first floor opening the front door there was Maggie sitting' on the stoop, twirling a whistle on a string.

T H E   E N D

In this picture, Ray and I are at the Hudson fishing before his passing. He catches me trying to put my two fingers behind his head. I miss him greatly.

Two doves released by children over St. Peter's Square Sunday in the name of world peace ran smack into two-winged bullies—a seagull and crow that attacked the birds in front of Pope Francis.

Ten of thousands watched as the angry birds dive-bombed the white doves—even stripping feathers off one—above Vatican City.

The pope had addressed the crowd from a window of the Apostolic Palace, calling for peace in the Ukraine, where antigovernment protests have turned deadly.

A boy and a girl then appeared at the pontiff's side and let the birds fly.

The doves escaped and flew off. (Post Wire Services)

ABOUT THE AUTHOR

A first-time author Danny Del Valle was born in New York City,raised in Spanish Harlem in his early years on hundred and 15th St. on Park Avenue,in the early 50s. Who is tired of hearing pigeons getting a bad rap,and wants to share his experience that he had when he was flying birds on the roof. He had posted pictures of his pigeon coop on the wall of his apartment. When someone visited for the first time, they would ask him about those pictures and when he told them about his pigeons and about his days on the roof, they all would say wow'. A few suggested he should write a story about it. not long ago he read a quote, saying a true sign of intelligence is not knowledge but imagination. Necessity is the mother of all invention.